Niwot

COLORADO

Niwot
COLORADO
BIRTH *of a* RAILROAD TOWN

Anne Quinby Dyni

Charleston   London

THE
History
PRESS

NORTHERN PLAINS
PUBLIC LIBRARY
Ault, Colorado

Published by The History Press
Charleston, SC 29403
www.historypress.net

Copyright © 2011 by Anne Quinby Dyni
All rights reserved

Depot photo courtesy of the Niwot Historical Society.

First published 2011

Manufactured in the United States

ISBN 978.1.60949.358.5

Library of Congress Cataloging-in-Publication Data

Dyni, Anne.
Niwot, Colorado : birth of a railroad town / Anne Quinby Dyni.
p. cm.
Summary: Newspaper articles written for the Left hand valley courier for fourteen years,
beginning in 1997.
Includes index.
ISBN 978-1-60949-358-5
1. Niwot (Colo.)--History. 2. Railroads--Colorado--Niwot--History. 3. Niwot (Colo.)--
Economic conditions. 4. Niwot (Colo.)--Social life and customs. 5. Niwot (Colo.)--Social
conditions. I. Left hand valley courier. II. Title.
F784.N59D95 2011
978.8'63--dc23
2011023104

CONTENTS

Contents

CONTENTS

ACKNOWLEDGEMENTS

Niwot, Colorado: Birth of a Railroad Town is a collection of seventy-six newspaper articles written over a period of fourteen years. It was 1997 when I began writing a history column called "Yesterday's News" for the fledgling local newspaper, the *Left Hand Valley Courier*. My assignment was to write about the history of Niwot, the Left Hand Valley and the railroad, without which Niwot would not exist. Little had been written about Niwot and its people, but there were many descendants of early settlers still living nearby. I wish to acknowledge those individuals for sharing their personal stories and family photographs, which helped to piece together many details of Niwot and the Left Hand Valley.

Thanks to the *Courier* founders, Bruce Warren (still its managing editor), Mary Wolbach Lopert (senior editor), Vicki Maurer (news and records editor), Karen Copperberg (website manager), Selene Hall (business manager), Ron Goodman (resident cartoonist) and Lori Lindemann for allowing me to reprint these articles for a new audience.

Thank you, also, to the Niwot Historical Society, which permitted me to include many of the historical images that accompanied the original newspaper articles. Its vast photograph collection is a valuable asset to the Niwot community. Additional photographs are attributed to individuals who shared their family stories during past interviews.

Thanks, also, to my husband, John, whose patience, expertise and encouragement are greatly appreciated.

INTRODUCTION

The small community of Niwot is located in the Left Hand Valley northeast of Boulder, Colorado. It was founded several years after the Pikes Peak Gold Rush of 1859. But unlike the earlier settlements of Boulder, Valmont, Burlington and Pella, which were located along major streams, Niwot was a railroad town.

The Left Hand Valley was settled by the time Porter Hinman platted it in 1875. Homesteaders had already laid claim to the fertile soil and flowing streams that were home to the Southern Arapaho Indians prior to the gold rush. Although their leader, Chief Niwot (meaning "Left Hand"), welcomed the first prospectors to the valley, he knew that his people would soon be forced aside as settlement continued.

The picturesque valley also beckoned to many disillusioned miners who had come west to seek their fortunes in the gold camps. They recognized its potential for growing food and feed for the hundreds of men and pack animals working in the mines above Boulder.

With a wealth of minerals from the Gold Hill mining district and a growing agricultural industry on the plains, the only ingredient that Boulder County lacked was a railroad. Laying track for the Colorado Central Railroad in 1873, which ultimately connected Denver with the Union Pacific Railroad in Wyoming, literally paved the way for Niwot's settlement.

Part I

EARLY SETTLEMENT OF THE LEFT HAND VALLEY

A FATEFUL DAY

On the surface, Sylvanus Budd was typical of the settlers who homesteaded in the Left Hand Valley in the 1860s. Yet, through the eyes of his seven-year-old neighbor, Budd was a man of almost mythical stature.

"He was an old Civil War veteran, and he was a blackjack player," Gilbert Hutchins recalled. "He'd won a lot of gold in the army, and they said he had one of those old silk hats full of gold coins when he came here."

In reality, Budd came to the gold fields of Colorado to seek his fortune in 1860. If he had any gold when he arrived in the Left Hand Valley, it was probably what little he had found in Black Hawk or Central City.

He took up land along Left Hand Creek, which today borders the Niwot cemetery on Nimbus Road. When the Jerome Gould family settled just to the east of the Budd ranch, a close relationship developed between the two men.

Evan Gould described Budd and his grandfather as good friends who collaborated on the creation of the Niwot cemetery in 1883. When Jerome deeded a portion of his land for the cemetery, Sylvanus donated and built the fence around it.

Both men raised cattle and maintained a branding corral on the north end of the Budd property. Each summer, Budd drove the cattle north into Wyoming to grazing land they had purchased between Cheyenne and Laramie.

Sylvanus Budd was a bachelor when he arrived in Colorado, but in the 1870s, he married Samantha Severens. Together they raised two daughters, Rose and Katie. When Katie married, she settled down nearby on acreage

Sylvanus Budd was a member of
the Colorado Territorial House
of Representatives in the 1870s.
Both he and his wife, Samantha,
are buried in the Niwot cemetery
on Nimbus Road. *Courtesy of
Niwot Historical Society.*

given to her by her father. Rose, however, was retarded and remained at
home under her mother's watchful eye.

Samantha refused to accompany her husband on his Wyoming cattle
drives, although he sometimes stayed away for months. Tragically, the long,
lonely wait and her constant anxiety about Rose took their toll. Although
Gilbert didn't witness the event that took Samantha's life, his mother's
description continued to haunt him.

"One day when my mother was hanging clothes," he recalled, "Mrs.
Budd come out of the house with a can full of coal oil. She walked over near
the orchard and poured it all over herself and set a match to it." Although
Gilbert's mother was severely burned while trying to save her, Samantha
died shortly afterward. She was fifty-six years old.

Rose was committed to the Colorado state mental hospital in Pueblo, and
Sylvanus was left with only the hired man and his family, which included
Gilbert, his siblings and his mother. The Hutchins family remained on the
Budd ranch for only four more years before leaving for a Mormon settlement
near Delta. It was there, many years later, that Gilbert tape-recorded his
memories of the Left Hand Valley and the star-crossed Budd family.

ALVAH DODD'S LEGACY

The stately Dodd barn and farmhouse on Niwot Road and North Seventy-third Street are impressive symbols of Boulder County's agricultural heritage. As countless farm buildings and silos disappear each year, homesteads such as this are even more appreciated.

Alvah Dodd Sr. came to the Left Hand Valley from Iowa in 1880, at the age of twenty-three. His older brother, Barnett, had come west years before to mine gold near Central City. Several other families were farming along Left Hand Creek when Alvah arrived. Sylvanus Budd, Porter Hinman and Jerome Gould were among the first white men to settle there.

Alvah courted Gould's eldest daughter, Della, and the two were married in 1885. Their first home, a modest frame structure, remains on the property, serving today as an outbuilding. By 1897, the family had outgrown their little house, so work began on the two-story brick home still standing under towering trees planted over a century ago. Eventually, this home was expanded to accommodate the couple's fourteen children. Four had died in infancy.

The huge barn that dominates the landscape today was built in 1914. The lower level housed twenty horses, and cattle were sheltered in a lean-to on the north side.

For several years, Alvah served as president of the Niwot State Bank. His son, Guy, was cashier when the bank folded in 1931. After their father's death, his sons John, Hugh and Alvah Jr. (the "h" was later dropped) continued to farm the land and purchased nearly two hundred additional acres.

Evan Gould often helped the brothers drive their cattle to the loading pens beside the Niwot depot. "There were enough for three or four carloads," he recalled. "It's about thirty head to a car."

World War II put a strain on farmers in Boulder County. As young men enlisted in the armed services, few were left to work the land. Alvah Dodd Jr. was able to raise sugar beets one final year by transporting German prisoners of war from the detention camp in Longmont to work in his fields. His wife, Beth, drove to the Great Western Sugar Company dormitories at Third and Kimbark Streets each morning to pick up twenty prisoners and their guards. "They brought their lunches into our front yard to eat," Beth explained, "and we furnished them something to drink."

In February 1999, the Dodd family entered into an agreement with Boulder County that guarantees the preservation of their historic property. The county purchased 243 acres, while 95 acres west of Seventy-third

The Dodd family posed beside their brick farmhouse in 1905. Getting their many children and the family dog ready to be photographed was quite an accomplishment. *Courtesy of Niwot Historical Society.*

Street were retained by other heirs. Dodd Lake, which lies west of the old homestead, was also purchased with all of its water rights.

A marker detailing the history of the Dodd family stands on the north shore of the lake. Alvah Dodd's descendants have thus ensured that his respect for the land and his contribution to the agricultural history of the Left Hand Valley will continue.

DOG DAYS OF SUMMER

Hot summer days are still with us, and it's refreshing to cool down with a tall glass of ice water. Looking back to about 1900, however, pouring that iced drink wasn't quite as easy as it is today. Enjoying ice in August meant harvesting it many months earlier, when the reservoirs were still frozen. Those were the days when six-foot ice saws were used to cut ice blocks, which were then loaded onto wagons and hauled to the nearest icehouse for storage.

Early Settlement of the Left Hand Valley

August Berhmann described the ice harvests of his youth. "First, we'd cut a hole in the ice. Then we'd take our ice saw and saw the blocks," he explained. "Then we'd take the ice tongs, grab the ice and pull it out. Depending on how hard the winter was, the ice could be six to eight inches thick."

According to early interviews, a typical ice block measured twenty-one inches square by eight inches thick. Thinner ice on the lakes couldn't withstand the weight of the men, horses and wagons needed to block and haul it away. If it was too thick, the blocks were difficult to handle.

Boulder County had many commercial icehouses in 1900. Almost every town had one nearby. Pete Peterson's pond and icehouse supplied ice to Lafayette. In Boulder, the Hygienic Ice Company maintained an icehouse at Twenty-first and Spruce Streets, where the Spruce swimming pool now stands. William Dickens maintained an icehouse on his property south of Longmont, where he stored ice harvested from local reservoirs. And in Niwot, farmers and grocers cut ice from Dodd Lake, to be hauled to their own icehouses for storage.

Like a pied piper, an ice wagon attracted children as it passed through neighborhoods. Dorothy Woodbury recalled that the driver "was very kind to us and gave us chunks of ice so we could munch on it." Elizabeth Farrow added, "If there were any little chips in [the wagon], you could help yourself."

Customers posted signs in their front windows indicating how many pounds they needed that day: 25#, 50#, 75# or 100#. The iceman then carried each order to the back porch and placed it directly into the icebox. A drip pan underneath caught the water as the ice melted. "My dad bored a hole in the back porch floor," said Dee Demmon. "If the pan ran over, [the water] went outdoors instead of all over the porch."

There were few ice deliveries to rural homes, however. Farmers either bought ice in town or harvested their own and stored it in a shed or barn. Irene Lybarger explained the process her father used. "My dad said that they put about two inches of sawdust between blocks, then put one block on top of the other. That way," she said, "it would keep all summer long." Sawdust was readily available from numerous sawmills operating in the foothills at that time.

As for pouring an icy beverage in the early 1900s, Mary Hummel Wells cautioned, "We always had ice right through the summer. But it wasn't sanitary, so we couldn't use it in drinks or anything like that."

You Can't Get There from Here

Many of us complain from time to time about traffic congestion and the deteriorating condition of our local roads. But have you ever stopped to consider who laid out those roads in the first place?

Try to visualize Boulder County in the 1860s, when rutted wagon trails were the only way to get from here to there. Those early routes were carved out by hundreds of miners and settlers arriving daily by wagon train, by stagecoaches carrying mail and passengers and by freight wagons bringing supplies from the Midwest to the early settlements of Burlington, Pella, Valmont and Boulder. It would be another twenty-five years before the county designated the Denver-Laramie stagecoach road a public highway. Today, that route follows U.S. Highway 287 through Boulder County from north of Broomfield to the Larimer County line north of Longmont.

Almost all the narrow canyon roads leading to the gold camps of Gold Hill, Central City and Black Hawk were built by private road companies, and all were vulnerable to rock slides or washouts.

Everything, whether on two legs, four legs or wheels, was charged a toll to use these private roads, and fees were collected at tollhouses located at either end. Passage over the Bear Canyon Road south of Boulder cost a man ten cents to walk beside his pack mule. Those mounted on horseback paid another twenty cents. Herds of horses, mules or cattle cost their drover a nickel a head, while sheep, goats and pigs passed through for just two cents apiece.

Overseers were appointed to maintain each Boulder County road district. Neighbors depended on them to keep the roads clear of rocks and snow. Heavy snows could quickly isolate ranchers and farmers if roads weren't cleared promptly. Wayne Arbuthnot described riding to Bader School as his father plowed through the drifts with an "A" hitched behind his road grader. He and his friends sat on the cross member of the A-shaped plow as it inched its way along the roads west of Niwot. Their added weight actually helped it to cut through the drifts more efficiently.

Proceedings from early Boulder County commissioner meetings often included discussions of proposed county roads. In December 1883, Hiram Prince petitioned the commissioners to open a road past his property southeast of Niwot. To complete the project, over a mile of old fencing was removed and new fencing installed. The purchase of the necessary rights of way brought the total cost of the three-mile section of road to $322.

Today, most county roads follow the section lines that originally separated homestead properties. Most were narrow dirt paths until well into the twentieth century and presented formidable challenges to the growing number of automobiles. Many farmers still recall hitching their teams to the bumpers of Model Ts to free them from the mud. So, the next time you feel a road complaint welling up inside, think again and count your blessings.

What's in a Name?

How did Gunbarrel Hill get its name? No one knows for sure, but the answer may lie in local legends. Some say it was when the Throndson family traded a shotgun for land near Niwot Road and Ninety-fifth Street. But the name probably came from the parallel ruts of a wagon trail extending along the crest of the hill between Valmont to the west and Burlington to the east. This became a well-traveled road in the 1860s.

Aside from gold camps in the foothills, there were few settlements in Boulder County at that time. Boulder City was the first, established as a supply town for miners. Farther to the east, Valmont and Burlington existed primarily to support the rapidly growing farming population. Pella, south of today's Hygiene, was settled along St. Vrain Creek, where John Davis's mill ground wheat into flour for early settlers.

Until the Boulder Valley Railroad was extended to Boulder City in 1873, local commerce was dependent on stagecoaches and freighters to deliver passengers and supplies from the States. Throughout the 1860s, stagecoaches on the Overland Stage Line traveled from Denver to Laramie and Salt Lake City along the eastern edge of Boulder County. Fresh teams were provided at "swing stations" located every twelve miles. At fifty-mile intervals, there were "home stations" where teams, as well as drivers, were replaced, and passengers could obtain food and lodging. Burlington was the site of the first home station north of Denver. There, Mary Allen provided travelers with sumptuous meals of soup; buffalo, antelope or deer; fresh bread; vegetables prepared with salt pork; pastries; and coffee—all for $1.50.

From Burlington, a branch headed west across Gunbarrel Hill to Valmont and Boulder City. Straight as the barrel of a gun, the road stopped first at Tommy Jones's Valmont House Hotel and stage station along Ferry Street in Valmont. Built before sawmills were introduced in the county, Jones used whipsawn lumber, cutting each log into boards by hand with a two-man saw. His wife, described as a large masculine woman, provided meals for travelers at her Valmont House Hotel.

After the stagecoach was replaced by a railroad, Emma Doud Gould (standing at the far right) managed the old Valmont House Hotel as a boardinghouse for local stone quarry workers. *Courtesy of George Sawhill.*

Years of dust storms and cultivation have erased all signs of the old wagon road, although old-timers say that ruts were faintly visible as recently as the 1940s. Burlington, which once stood on the south side of St. Vrain Creek, is gone as well. It was absorbed by Longmont over a century ago. Valmont, however, still lies north of Valmont Butte, with a few original buildings still standing. Among them, the Tommy Jones Hotel and stage station has survived countless floods to survive as the largest remaining whipsawn structure in Boulder County.

GOOD TO THE LAST DROP

With watering restrictions again in place in the summer of 2003, many homeowners were concerned about adequately maintaining their healthy lawns and gardens. While these inconveniences affect the cosmetic aspects of our urban lifestyles, we tend to forget those whose livelihoods depend on a steady supply of water.

Ever since 1859, farmers and ranchers along the Front Range have tapped into the major streams pouring out of the foothills and onto the plains.

Early Settlement of the Left Hand Valley

Settlers who came from more humid climates quickly learned that spring rains invariably gave way to the hot, dry days of summer and that their crops and livestock could not survive without a dependable backup water supply.

They soon realized that the traditional concepts of American water law did not apply to lands west of the 100th meridian. The Riparian Rights doctrine practiced in the eastern states allowed for only limited use of rivers and streams by adjacent property owners. The primary goal was to protect a river's flow to enable navigation and to ensure water power for the operation of flour and sawmills along its banks. Successful agriculture back East was dependent almost entirely on rainfall.

But when Colorado attained statehood in 1876, the Doctrine of Prior Appropriation was included in its charter. The western version of water law, simply interpreted, meant *first in time, first in right*. Those who were first to adjudicate their water rights in the courts were allowed to take water before those who filed later. By 1899, Colorado ranked first in the nation in the number of irrigated acres.

Both St. Vrain and Left Hand Creeks empty onto the plains of northern Boulder County. Left Hand Ditch Company, which controls all of the flow from Left Hand Creek, was issued its first water decree in 1863 and provides irrigation water for much of the Niwot area.

Protection of their water rights occasionally brought out the worst in people. Issues that today are handled by attorneys in court were once settled in the fields by the farmers themselves. To counteract a neighbor's continual practice of plugging his head gate with weeds in order to divert the ditch water onto his own fields, one farmer simply placed a beehive on it. Merchant Charles Wright of Niwot described a fistfight that quickly escalated into dueling shovels. "It ended abruptly," he said, "when one of the farmers was struck in the ribs and fell to the ground." Perhaps that explains why early water commissioners wore badges and carried guns.

When the late Lee Forsythe was asked if new housing developments around Niwot had an impact on his job as a ditch rider, he responded with a resounding "yes." He explained that new homeowners are often unaware that easements along ditches were created to facilitate ditch maintenance and repair. "When people buy property," he explained, "they don't have any idea what irrigation is and will invariably want to build a fence along the bank or plant a lot of trees there."

Today, as newcomers move to the Front Range, the issue of water rights continues to have an impact on the livelihood of the county's agricultural families.

Women's Work

The concept of women in business is hardly new, although the number of women working outside the home today far exceeds that of a century ago. Before 1900, working women usually ran boardinghouses, taught school or cooked and ironed for others. Yet the 1896 Boulder County Business Directory listed only one professional woman in Niwot: Mary Jones, housekeeper

An examination of school records, however, reveals the whole story. Most teachers employed by Niwot's School District #7 were women—and often from local families.

Cordia Clifford had been widowed and then married to a man who did little to support her and their children. In order to provide food for the table and pay for therapeutic mineral baths for her husband, Frank, Cordia became postmaster in the little red building beside Nelson Hall. Helping her with the rural mail delivery was Luella Blanton. Luella had never intended to become a mailman, but circumstances dictated that she assume her husband's job after his fatal accident. He was killed in 1916, when his horse panicked during a severe hailstorm and pinned him underneath his mail wagon.

Before 1910, all of Niwot's postmasters were men. Each conducted postal business from behind a small counter at the rear of his store. But from 1911 to 1922, a series of women held the position. The first, Julia Stockley, worked in Niwot's first official post office building on Murray Street. Her picture hangs above the counter in the current post office, which was built on the same site in 1967.

As more businesses appeared along Second Avenue, the number of working women increased. Louise and Lee Newell came to Niwot in the early 1920s. They purchased Cordia Clifford's little red post office and turned it into a grocery store with a postal counter inside. Their ad in a 1923 *Niwot Tribune* listed candies, coffee, cigars and school supplies available in what they called "The Post Office Store." Louise, in partnership with her husband, Lee, became Niwot's next postmaster.

When William and Mattie Sutton purchased the Livingston Hotel across the street in about 1920, Mattie hired Naomi Tilbury's mother, then a young girl, to clean rooms. William shoed horses in the empty lot next door. His tragic death at the heels of a client's horse propelled Mattie into sole ownership of the hotel, a position she held for the next several years.

Delia Wilson had one of the more physically challenging occupations in town. While her crippled husband, Will, served as station agent and telegrapher, she managed platform duties at the train depot.

Delia Wilson waits for the morning train beside a station platform wagon loaded with fresh milk, eggs and produce destined for market. As the result of a childhood accident, her husband, Will, had only one leg, which considerably limited his duties as station agent. *Courtesy of Niwot Historical Society.*

Down the street at the *Niwot Tribune* office, Florence Hayes served as associate editor of her husband Edward's newspaper.

Belle Dodd clerked for Hogsett's Lumber and Mercantile until resigning to keep the books for the place where many in her family were already employed.

Today, many Niwot businesses are owned by women. They are continuing a trend that began, albeit slowly, more than a century ago.

St. Vrain Valley Pioneers

The word *pioneer* has been loosely interpreted by historians over the years. But to founders of the St. Vrain Valley Pioneers Association, the term originally applied to families who settled in Boulder County prior to 1871. This cutoff date was chosen in order to deliberately exclude members of the Chicago Colony who had founded Longmont that same year. The requirement was strictly enforced until the 1960s, when pioneer families arriving as late as 1879 were at last permitted to join.

The change came only after some of the more inflexible members of the organization passed away. Two in particular, James Forsythe and Nimrod Henry of Niwot, were perhaps the most dogged in their opposition. Nimrod was known to friends and family as a man of "determined nature," whose usual response to a disagreement was to turn on his heels and walk away. But in this case, he clung adamantly to his opinion and refused to give in.

Established in 1904, the Pioneer Association was the brainchild of Longmont resident Lydia Franklin Secor and others. A printed invitation to its organizational meeting was sent to all qualified families. Among those gathered in Longmont's Dickens Opera House that summer day were many from the Niwot area, including, of course, Nimrod Henry.

No charter has ever been located, although fragile minutes books dating from 1904 still exist. Those reveal that the founding members established far-reaching boundaries for membership eligibility. The original description stated that "all of Boulder County and surrounding area" actually included a large region bounded by the Poudre River on the north, the Platte River to the east and the south and west boundaries of Boulder County.

The original membership list totaled 476 families, but as with many other historic organizations today, the lack of interest by younger descendants and

You can see it in their faces—the pride that comes from being a pioneer. Of the sixteen individuals pictured here in 1946, more than a dozen were over the age of eighty. *Courtesy of Niwot Historical Society.*

the steady passing of their elders threaten the very existence of the St. Vrain Valley Pioneers Association.

In spite of this, families still meet annually for fellowship and to honor those who have died the previous year. Inez Sawdey, herself a pioneer descendant from Longmont, prepares memorials for the annual meetings at the Hygiene Methodist Church every fall. The year 2004 marked the 100th anniversary of the association, and the annual meeting drew a larger crowd than usual.

Frontier Brides

While June has long been considered the month for weddings, marriage traditions have changed considerably in the past one hundred years. And as some of the following stories illustrate, honeymoons were often considered impractical.

Nineteenth-century brides usually married between the ages of sixteen and eighteen after brief engagements. If a girl was not wed by age twenty-five, she was considered an old maid.

After their Iowa wedding in 1861, Jerome Gould planned to take his wife, Amy, to the gold fields of Black Hawk, Colorado. Amy's sister, however, called Jerome "the biggest fool that ever lived" and persuaded her to stay behind. Finally, against her family's wishes, Amy joined Jerome when he returned for her the following year. The Goulds eventually purchased a homestead in the Left Hand Valley, where their descendants still live today.

Euphrasia Gilson was seventeen when she and her husband left Kansas Territory by oxen and covered wagon. Although they anticipated hardships along the way, they never expected that one of their oxen would be bitten by a rattlesnake and their milk cow would have to pull the wagon the rest of the way.

The hardships and austere living conditions of frontier life required painful adjustments for all who came west. Add to this the culture shock experienced by young brides who came from as far away as Europe and Asia. Kunihei Miyasaki arrived in Boulder County from Japan in about 1920 to work as a field laborer. He returned home just long enough to marry a young woman chosen by his family to be his bride. With little education and no knowledge of the English language, Sono Miyasaki joined her husband in the simple tenant house he had provided for her near Erie. The language and cultural barriers she encountered were considerable. She never ventured far beyond her Japanese community along Isabelle Road, and she never learned to speak English.

One of the more lively traditions for newlyweds in the 1920s and 1930s was the chivaree. "That was a social event," Rose Kelsey laughed. "When you got married, you'd better figure on cigars and candy for the whole neighborhood," she explained. "We just barely had enough money to buy candy for all the people we knew was going to be there."

Sure enough, soon after Rose and Charles Kelsey returned from their wedding in the Denver courthouse, neighbors along Ninety-fifth Street announced their late-night visit in true chivaree fashion. After much shouting, drumming and clashing of pots and pans, they were invited inside. Rose smiled as she recalled that night. "We had a houseful," she said.

In Niwot, a groom was expected to push his bride up and over the sugar beet ramp along Murray Street in a wheelbarrow. Alvah Dodd was huffing and puffing by the time he reached the top with Beth Conilogue, his new bride. Sadly, this tradition disappeared in the 1940s, when the beet ramp was removed.

Luther and Lizzie Caywood were fondly referred to by friends as "Mutt and Jeff." *Courtesy of Lois Caywood Graves.*

SARSAPARILLA AND WORM SYRUP

Mail-order medicines listed in the 1897 Sears catalogue read like the inventory of a medieval drug dispensary. From Nerve and Brain Pills to Toothache Wax, there was something for everyone. Worm cakes were guaranteed to remove parasites from adult innards, while a product called Pink Pills for Pale People promised to cure just about everything else.

Despite those bizarre-sounding concoctions, medicines had come a long way since the early days of western migration. Of the nearly 300,000 pioneers who crossed the Great Plains between 1840 and 1860, about 1 in 10 died along the way. The majority of them succumbed to measles, typhoid, dysentery and cholera. Stopping overnight where previous wagon trains had camped only exacerbated the spread of those diseases.

Although doctors knew little about cholera, they correctly associated it with contaminated water. The wells on many homesteads were often located near corrals or a short distance from an outhouse. "Under those circumstances," one country doctor remarked, "how can it fail to become contaminated?"

As settlement of Boulder County began in the early 1860s, a long list of diseases challenged the health of the pioneers. Tetanus, contracted through splinters or rusty nails, could be fatal. Botulism from improperly canned food threatened families as well.

It wasn't until 1910 that Niwot's first doctor arrived in town. When the last doctor left in 1928, residents needing medical attention had to travel to Longmont or Boulder for treatment or hospitalization. For convenience as well as cost, some families reverted back to reliance on home remedies. Although memories of foul-smelling asafetida bags, castor oil and kerosene-soaked sugar cubes still haunt many old-timers, those home remedies worked amazingly well.

Bites from rabid animals posed another risk. In 1917, nine train passengers pausing in Niwot were bitten by a stray dog. The unfortunate victims continued on home to Denver, where they were treated for three weeks with daily injections of rabies vaccine.

Rattlesnakes were a constant hazard for families near the foothills. Venomous snakebites were so common that some folks carried small bottles of turpentine in their pockets for emergency treatment. Irene Smith described arming herself with a hoe each morning as she walked with her siblings to the Potato Hill School near Table Mountain.

Some folks may recall the patent medicine shows of their childhood. Behind the hype and showmanship, patent medicines were generally nothing

Dr. Dasef, Niwot's first doctor, set up practice on Second Avenue at Franklin Street. There, he dispensed medicine at the front counter and treated patients in an examining room at the rear of the building. *Courtesy of Niwot Historical Society.*

more than a mixture of vegetable root compounds and generous amounts of alcohol. Pinkham's Vegetable Compound contained 21 percent alcohol, and Hostetter's Celebrated Stomach Bitters had 44 percent. Chuck Waneka of Lafayette remembered the antics of fast-talking salesmen as they played the small-town crowds. Even at a young age, he suspected that the rattlesnake repeatedly biting the salesman on cue probably had no fangs.

MOVING TO SUMMER RANGE

The term *cattle drive* evokes images of TV's *Lonesome Dove* or early Hollywood westerns. However, Colorado Territory saw very few cattle drives of that magnitude, and the herds that did pass through traveled far to the east of the foothills.

Early Settlement of the Left Hand Valley

According to Martin Parsons, a stagecoach driver and Boulder's first park ranger, Texas had almost four million cattle in 1860. With no market for the beef, thousands were slaughtered for their hides and tallow. But the discovery of gold near Black Hawk, Central City and Gold Hill in 1858 brought an influx of prospectors to the area, thus creating a market for beef. Only a few longhorns were sold in the gold camps, however, because local ranchers and businessmen saw the opportunity to meet the demand themselves.

Many returned to the Midwest to purchase herds. J.J. Beasley was only twenty-one when he undertook the first of four trips back to Missouri to buy cattle. According to his grandson Cecil Beasley of Longmont, "It took Grandfather about six months to travel, and it was only on the last trip that he had a horse to ride."

Herefords and shorthorns were among the more popular breeds at that time. They were superior to the light-bodied, long-legged Texas cattle whose ungainly horns measured five feet or more between tips.

Boundary fences enclosed entire groups of farms in the 1860s, so neighboring herds often grazed together. Because the cattle intermingled, branding took place every spring, prior to moving them to summer range. Large herds were driven up Left Hand, St. Vrain and Boulder Canyons

There were 625 brands registered in Boulder County by 1880. Catherine Caywood from Niwot was the first woman to record her brand, described in the state brand book as a letter "C" on the left hip. *Courtesy of Lois Caywood Graves.*

along early toll roads, where farmers were charged a fee for each head of livestock. In 1873, the Boulder County commissioners levied a uniform toll of twenty cents per saddle horse and five cents for each loose horse, mule or cow.

Mary Hummel Wells recalled the cattle drives of the 1930s and 1940s, when she helped her father move their livestock from Valmont into the hills above Boulder. "At spring roundup, we would brand and de-horn, then let the cows settle in for about two or three days." She and her father then herded them to their corrals near Broadway and Lee Hill Road. "Lee Hill Road was not the boulevard that it is now," Mary said. "It was a one-lane road."

In the fall, the cattle were driven back down the canyons and separated out to their respective farms. Many early farmers and ranchers did not feed livestock through the winter months but instead sent them directly to the stockyards in Denver.

Bushels of Grasshoppers

Was your garden devastated by grasshoppers this past summer? Did they nibble the tassels off your sweet corn or shred your favorite flower bed? Well, unless your livelihood centers on the success of your garden, the following historical account should put your loss in perspective.

In the mid-1870s, farmers in Boulder County battled swarms of grasshoppers so pervasive that it is difficult today to comprehend their magnitude. In his memoirs, Ernest Pease described the event from his childhood: "I recall with a special clearness the dulling of the sky as if a great cloud were passing overhead. But unlike the smooth texture of the cloud, the incipient darkness was filled with a moving mass of dark specks."

Ernest and his brother, Clarence, were filled with wonder and excitement at the spectacle. They grabbed boards and began batting at each speck as it fell, counting the number they actually hit. Soon, the hoppers were descending in such numbers that the boys gave up and simply gazed in astonishment.

The insects invading the Front Range that summer were Rocky Mountain locust, or *Melanoplus spretus*, a form of long-winged migratory grasshopper. By 1875, their presence had become a familiar sight to settlers throughout the West. Those who believed the swarms would not return the following year were wrong. When spring arrived, farmers plowing their fields unearthed millions of eggs laid the previous year. Those that hatched that spring caused comparatively minor damage, however, and folks began to breathe a bit easier. Little did they know that another wave was winging its way from the Northwest toward the foothills of Colorado.

In a frantic attempt to fight the onslaught, farmers opened up their irrigation ditches and flooded their fields. Miraculously, within a few days, practically no hoppers remained. They had not been eradicated, however— just relocated.

Many were sighted in the mountains as well. In 1876, the *Central City Register* reported clouds of grasshoppers "covering the streets, sidewalks, and even the garments of pedestrians." Soon, snow banks on the high mountain peaks were covered with decaying grasshoppers, filling the air with a putrid odor.

Even the railroads were inconvenienced by the insects. They were so thick on the rails that the huge steam engines could not pull their loads on even the slightest grade. Their massive wheels spun aimlessly on the oily carcasses until sand was applied to the tracks.

But by 1877, local farmers had begun to design machines to save their crops from devastation. James King invented a two-wheeled hopper-dozer, which was pulled through infested fields by teams of horses. As it rolled forward, its fourteen-foot apron swept up the hoppers and directed them toward a spinning fan resting between the wheels. The suction was so powerful that stones, as well as insects, were thrown into the oil-filled drums mounted underneath.

As horses pulled this hopper-dozer through the field, the grasshoppers flew up, hit the canvas backsplash and then fell into vats of oil that stretched the entire width of the apparatus. *Courtesy Colorado Historical Society.*

In spite of farmers' ingenuity, however, nothing succeeded until the introduction of hydrocarbon-based insecticides after World War II. Occasional invasions still occur, but none with the intensity and devastation of past assaults. Those migratory insects are said to be extinct—their last Colorado flight having been recorded in 1877.

EARLY POST OFFICES

Although frontier newspapers kept settlers reasonably informed of current events, it was personal letters that tied pioneer families to their loved ones back East. The delivery of mail was eagerly awaited by everyone.

Until the arrival of two rail lines into Boulder County in 1873, however, settlers relied on the stagecoach for mail delivery. Local mail routes were established by men like Marinus Smith of Boulder, who operated the Marinus Express, a mail delivery and passenger stagecoach line between Boulder and Denver in the early 1860s. He charged fifty cents for each letter mailed to "the States."

As new communities appeared along the Front Range, requests poured into the U.S. Post Office Department for additional post office designations. The National Archives in Washington, D.C., retains the original applications, and Boulder's Carnegie Library for Local History houses copies of those pertinent to Boulder County.

From Tommy Jones's application for the Valmont Post Office in 1865, to Louis Nawatny's request for Louisville's post office in 1878, the documents read like history books. It was a challenge for a prospective postmaster to accurately complete the government form. Each proposed site had to be located on a grid, relying almost entirely on geographical landmarks, such as natural waterways and rock formations.

By the time Samuel Dobbins applied for the Niwot Post Office in 1874, the railroad was in operation. This made the site much easier to pinpoint. Since the town itself had not yet been platted, the application referred only to the railroad section house and the 150 rural families who would be served by the facility. After noting the proper section, township and range, additional details placed Niwot three-quarters of a mile south of Left Hand Creek and 150 feet west of the Colorado Central Railroad tracks.

Merchants often doubled as postmasters and placed postal boxes in the back of their dry goods stores or barbershops. The location of Niwot's post office changed several times over the years: the Bader Brothers Mercantile on

Julia Stockley was Niwot's postmaster from 1911 to 1914. She lived upstairs with her family on Murray Street while operating the post office on the ground floor. *Courtesy of Niwot Historical Society.*

Hinman Street, Cordia Clifford's building next to Nelson Hall, Julia Stockley's frame house on Murray Street, Reverend Taylor's grocery store, Eva Haddon's former Niwot State Bank building and the current post office on Murray Street.

Although incoming mailbags are no longer tossed from the train onto the depot platform each morning, and outgoing mail isn't hung from a pole to be snagged by an agile train employee, folks in Niwot still walk to the post office each day, stopping to visit with friends along the way.

Planting a Green Future

To the pioneer who set his gaze westward in the 1860s, Colorado Territory seemed like the Promised Land. Among those extolling its many attributes was William Byers, editor of Denver's *Rocky Mountain News*. Byers often devoted considerable space in his editorials to *boosterisms* to lure prospective settlers to the Front Range.

Other promoters included the Burlington Railroad, which published a brochure in 1887 entitled *Eastern Colorado: New Lands Now Being Opened Up.* It hoped to attract farmers and businessmen who would use its rail line to transport products to market. In the flowery prose of the day, it greatly exaggerated both the area's climate and its annual rainfall: "The climate is a glorious inspiration, an outpouring from the storehouse of nature's richest gifts. Water never fails here, but at all times furnishes an abundant supply."

The reality is, of course, that if all irrigation ditches and wells were removed from eastern Colorado today, it would soon revert to the landscape first encountered by settlers lured west by those misleading brochures more than 120 years ago.

The trek from Nebraska to the foothills of Boulder County crossed hundreds of miles of grassland with isolated trees and shrubs growing only along the rivers and streams. Many homesteaders, having been forewarned about the barren landscape, found room in their wagons for seedlings to landscape their new homes. Even the federal government encouraged tree cultivation by including a timber culture section in the Homestead Act of 1862. This allowed an additional ten acres of land but required that twenty-seven hundred trees be planted on each of those ten acres. At maturity or

On Arbor Day in 1912, students from the Davidson School at Ninety-fifth Street and Isabelle Road planted young trees in the schoolyard. Drive past the site today and see how much those seedlings have grown. *Courtesy of Rose Kelsey.*

before, they would conceivably provide wood for fence posts, shelter for wildlife and living windbreaks against the inevitable forces of nature.

A list of recommended timber trees was provided, not all of which were appropriate for Colorado's arid climate. Butternut, basswood, white willow, hickory and larch were far better suited to the Midwest than the high plains of Colorado Territory. As Mother Nature continually reminds us today, eastern Colorado experiences periods of extreme drought, flooding, wind and hail.

With a goal of continuing the cultivation of trees, Arbor Day was founded in Nebraska in 1872. The tradition was adopted by public schools ten years later, and today, almost every state in the Union celebrates by planting trees on the date they have chosen as Arbor Day. This can vary from January in Florida to April in Colorado.

Alice Steele Campion recalled that nothing would grow in the Ryssby schoolyard west of Niwot. "Arbor Day was always celebrated in those days, and trees were always planted," she said. "But it was such a dry and windy hill that nothing ever grew—only cactus."

THE FRONTIER SCHOOLTEACHER

As the doors close on schoolhouses for the summer and teachers take a well-earned rest, it's a good time to reflect on those who taught in the Left Hand Valley decades ago.

Working conditions in the early one-room schoolhouses were often arduous: the hours were long, and the pay was poor. Individual teachers were responsible for educating students in all eight grades, often constrained by a dearth of textbooks and supplies. Add to that the occasional four- or five-year-old who was sent to school with older siblings because (as Clancy Waneka expressed it) their "mother wanted an empty house so that she could get her work done more efficiently."

Salaries varied little between men and women. All were low—about forty-five dollars a month—although some teachers were paid an additional five dollars for janitorial duties. They had the choice of hauling firewood and drinking water into the classroom each morning or paying a student to do it for them. Young Ed Boden always arrived at school ahead of the other children. The teacher counted on him to have the building warm and the floor swept by the time classes began at nine o'clock. Mrs. Pease paid Ed five cents a day for his services, and he felt privileged to do those chores for her.

Each school was a separate district with its own three-member school board, usually composed of parents. Teachers were at the mercy of those parents, who ranged from progressive to conservative in their spending policies. For years, only unmarried women were hired and then burdened with unreasonable restrictions. Those in Allenspark, for instance, couldn't dress in bright colors, keep company with men or travel beyond the town limits without permission from the school board. Male teachers were allowed only one evening a week for courting purposes, providing they attended church regularly or taught a Sunday school class.

For female teachers just out of high school, disciplining older pupils could be difficult. The age difference was sometimes only a year or two. Colorado law dictated that students could be as young as six years or as old as twenty-one. Size and strength occasionally compensated for lack of teaching experience, however.

Mrs. Love, principal of the Niwot School in the early 1900s, was a huge woman who, according to Evan Gould, sprouted red spots on the back of her neck when she was riled. "She'd say, 'I'm gonna cut your tongue out and hang it on the clothesline to dry,' he chuckled. "And us kids believed her."

Another teacher developed a precision eraser pitch that could snap students to attention clear across the room. And when Mr. Oliver DeMott attempted to grab a pupil in the Valmont School, the boy attached himself so firmly to his desk that both he and the desk were unbolted from the floor.

Living conditions in smaller communities were sometimes so primitive that few teachers applied for positions there. In the mountain districts, pay was low, and available housing was often inferior. Those who were hired usually stayed only one year before moving elsewhere to a better job. Dee Demmon recalled waking up in the shack provided by the Magnolia school district to find the water in her washbowl frozen solid. And it was weeks before she became used to the sounds of packrats scurrying about inside the walls at night.

Teachers who couldn't easily commute from home stayed in boardinghouses, rented rooms or lived with local families. Often, the household with the most children enrolled in class became host family for the year. When the school board in Superior chose a needy family to board young Carrie Ewing for the school year, they spent her rent money for their own needs instead of providing her meals. Carrie was forced to sneak food into her room after weekend visits with her family.

Advancement for young teachers was earned by attending summer school classes at the University of Colorado or the State Teachers College in Greeley. Lifetime teaching certificates were awarded only with a college degree, and it wasn't until 1961 that such degrees were required of all Colorado teachers.

Part II

ESTABLISHING A RAILROAD TOWN

THE MAN WHO FOUNDED NIWOT

Many homesteaders had already settled in the Left Hand Valley north of Boulder by the time the town of Niwot was platted. Among them was a man named Porter Hinman.

Hinman left his wife and family in Indiana in 1848 and headed west to seek his fortune during the California Gold Rush. He rejoined his family four years later but again headed west in the Pikes Peak Gold Rush of 1859. After several months, he returned home a second time. But having witnessed the demand for crops to feed the miners and their pack animals, he realized that his calling was in farming, not prospecting.

Once again, he traveled to Colorado, this time with his eldest son, Mortimer, to claim eighty acres of prime farmland in the Left Hand Valley. Within a year, his entire family had joined him, and his landholdings soon increased to four hundred acres, all of which lay northwest of today's Niwot Road and Seventy-ninth Street.

In 1873, the Colorado Central Railroad completed its route from Denver to Boulder and was preparing to extend its tracks all the way to Longmont. This required obtaining easements all along the fifteen-mile route. The route did not follow section lines but cut diagonally through the fields and pastures of many homesteaders in the Left Hand Valley. By the end of the year, all the necessary easements had been acquired and the laying of track had begun.

The railroad was a marketing windfall for those already farming in the area—a fact not lost on Hinman. In 1875, he and Ambrose Murray of Boulder drew up plans for a town at the site of the railroad section house located halfway between Boulder and Longmont. They named the town for Southern Arapaho chief Niwot, whose people had hunted and camped in the valley years before prospectors arrived in the area.

Hinman and Murray immortalized themselves by giving their names to the streets along either side of the tracks. Hinman Street disappeared when the Diagonal Highway was built in the 1970s, but Murray Street exists to this day.

With construction of a depot, farmers were able to ship their milk, produce and livestock to markets in Longmont, Denver and beyond. Within a few years, several agriculture-related businesses were established in town, including a creamery, an alfalfa mill and a branch of the Longmont Farmers Mill.

Porter Hinman and his wife, Mary, left Boulder County sometime after 1880 and retired to the Hahn's Peak region of northwestern Colorado.

Porter T. Hinman was born in New York State in 1816. He was said to be a spiritualist who held séances in the family home on Seventy-third Street. *Courtesy of Niwot Historical Society.*

Although Hinman's name is still connected to the Hinman Ditch, which still flows underground through Niwot, it is the town itself that remains his greatest legacy.

OTHER SIDE OF THE TRACKS

When you stand at the west end of Second Avenue and look across the tracks, the view is spectacular. Had you stood in that same spot 120 years ago, both the sights and sounds would have been quite different.

The mountains were awe-inspiring because the absence of polluted air made them appear much closer than they do today. There was no Diagonal Highway and no traffic other than the occasional horse-drawn farm wagon or buggy. Second Avenue, then called Main Street, continued west across the tracks and beyond, connecting the residents of Niwot to the town's original business district.

You would have heard the sounds of livestock and poultry, the occasional steam whistle as a Colorado Central train pulled up to the depot and perhaps the clanking of a hammer striking the anvil in Jim Hood's blacksmith shop.

Just as Murray Street still parallels the east side of the tracks today, Hinman Street paralleled the west side. Named after Porter Hinman, who platted Niwot in 1875, Hinman Street was lined with small businesses. Few records remain of those early buildings, but historic photographs reveal stores and even a few residences tucked in among the trees. Although commercial businesses were listed in early regional directories, it is unlikely that the town constable, justice of the peace or the Niwot Building and Investment Company maintained offices in town. They probably conducted business from home.

Typical of the architecture of early western towns, the stores were wooden or brick, and many had false fronts. They catered primarily to the rural families living in the Left Hand Valley. Frank and George Bader's mercantile carried a large selection of hardware, groceries, clothing and farm implements. Frank was Niwot's postmaster, and since there was no post office building at that time, he distributed the daily mail from postal boxes in the back of his store.

Much of the day's activities centered on the blacksmith shop, where farmers gathered to swap stories while Jim Hood sharpened their plow blades or welded broken implements. Like several other shopkeepers in town, Hood possessed more than one skill. He was also listed in the Boulder City Directory as a carpenter.

Like most small-town general stores, Bill Buchert's Cash Department Store on Hinman Street carried groceries, clothing, shoes and hardware items. *Courtesy of Niwot Historical Society.*

The picturesque United Brethren Church was reminiscent of New England churches, and with its tall spire, it looked almost out of place in the field west of town. The entire building was eventually hauled into Niwot on skids after businesses began to move to the east side of the tracks in early 1900.

THE CAR COMES TO NIWOT

Imagine Niwot in 1910, when only horse-drawn wagons and buggies traveled the roads. Farmers hauled milk to the depot, sugar beet wagons headed for the beet dump along Murray Street and wagonloads of grain were delivered to the flour mill across the tracks.

The width of Second Avenue today attests to the fact that wagons and teams took up a fair amount of space when tied to the hitching posts in front of almost every business establishment.

Over the years, George Atkinson witnessed the decline of horse-drawn wagons and carriages as the first automobiles began to invade the roadways. In 1927, he built a garage, which shared a common wall with his blacksmith shop on Second Avenue. In addition to repairing broken plow blades, George began welding fenders and selling tires. His tools now included an acetylene torch and baling wire.

Gradually, more and more people purchased family automobiles. Even Clarence Conilogue, who was a familiar sight traveling down the road in his horse-drawn mail wagon, upgraded to a Model T in 1916. "Dad and I walked down the railroad tracks to Longmont to drive a Ford home," Clarence recalled. He alternated between the mail wagon and the car for five years before putting his old horse, Bill, out to pasture.

Evan Gould remembered when his father bought a Model T truck that "just run with pedals." Budd Conilogue convinced him to put a transmission in it, and after it was installed, Budd added a word of caution. "Now, whatever you do, don't get this thing out of gear 'cause you got no brakes." Evan laughed as he recalled hauling grain back to town from Gunbarrel Hill one day when the truck jumped out of gear. "Boy, down the road I come," he said, "and I coasted clear up to just about where Cottonwood Square [shopping center] is now. I don't know how fast it was a-goin', but it was a-goin'."

George Monthey opened an auto repair shop in what is now the Wise Buys building on Second Avenue and installed one of the first hand-operated gas

Although there were no car dealerships in Niwot, John Buckley sold automobiles from his farm on Eighty-third Street, just north of town. Representing a Boulder dealership, he brought one car at a time to display in his front yard. *Courtesy of Lula Mae James.*

pumps in town. Even though the Apex Refinery was just down the tracks at Sixty-third Street, Monthey purchased his gasoline from Denver because Apex did not sell to local merchants. There wasn't enough demand, they said. Although there were pumps at the refinery, the gasoline contained no additives and was usable only in low-compression engines like tractors.

Gradually, more gas stations opened in Niwot, but competition soon closed them down. Don Spangler closed his Texaco station on Second Avenue in 1948. "I only kept it open about eight months," he said. "It only took me eight months to go broke."

RAILROAD SECTION HOUSES

When the first railroads arrived in Colorado Territory in the early 1870s, there were only about forty struggling settlements along the Front Range. By 1890, however, nearly 350 railroad towns had appeared along the forty-five hundred miles of track crisscrossing the state.

In order to maintain and repair rail lines that passed through sparsely populated areas, the early railroad companies divided their routes into ten- to fifteen-mile-long sections. A foreman was assigned to each section to supervise needed maintenance with the help of repair crews.

In isolated areas, small and cheaply built section houses were built within the railroad right of way. These were modest one- or two-story frame structures with clapboard or board-and-batten sheathing and tin or shingled roofs. Although their simple architectural style varied from region to region, they generally resembled farmhouses. The smallest section houses had only a living room and bedroom, with a fireplace for warmth and cooking. Those built for families included a kitchen and an additional bedroom or two. The upper level, if there was one, served as a common sleeping area.

When the Colorado Central Railroad laid track through the Left Hand Valley in 1873, there were relatively few homesteaders living in the area. Niwot had not yet been platted, so the closest settlements along the route were Boulder and Longmont. Therefore, at a point halfway between those two communities, a section house called Modoc was built beside the tracks. Although there are no records to validate the exact year it was constructed, it appeared in several early Niwot photographs. It stood just south of Niwot Road, only a few yards west of the tracks.

Unfortunately, it is no longer standing and may have been among the many buildings removed when work began on the Diagonal Highway in 1957.

Family was important to Juan Apodaca and his wife. Their children and grandchildren spent considerable time together in the Niwot section house while Juan was foreman there. *Courtesy of Niwot Historical Society.*

For several years, maintenance crews were housed in modified boxcars parked behind the section house. But by the early 1900s, crewmen with families were renting homes in Niwot, while single workers boarded at the Livingston Hotel on Second Avenue.

Section foreman Juan Apodaca was transferred to Niwot from Trinidad, Colorado, in about 1920. He and his wife lived in Niwot's section house, while several of their children and grandchildren lived in town. Four of their grandchildren—John Montoya, Delia Montoya Hammons, Millie Montoya Rendon and Vidilia Montoya Rael—still visit Niwot from time to time and pay respects to family members buried in the Niwot cemetery.

NIWOT'S PIONEER CEMETERY

There are many pioneer cemeteries in Boulder County, both on the plains and in the mountains. Some have been absorbed into neighboring communities, while others, which were created for family burials, remain isolated on private land.

Such a place was the Niwot cemetery. Jerome and Amy Gould had settled along Seventy-third Street, north of Nimbus Road, in 1862. In 1881, their thirteen-year-old son, Ernest, died of appendicitis. When they buried him in the Burlington cemetery, eight miles to the east, Amy was unable to visit his grave as often as she wished. She asked Jerome to find an appropriate grave site on their own land.

Lying along Left Hand Creek, the Gould farm was blessed with fertile soil. But the southern portion of the property along Nimbus Road was underlain by a shallow layer of shale. Because it was unfit for cultivation, approximately two acres on this dry knoll were chosen for the family cemetery. Years later, Evan Gould complained that the shale layer made grave digging there almost impossible. "You might as well be digging in cement," he used to say. "It took six people almost all day to dig one grave."

The first burial was that of young Ernest, whose body had been exhumed from the Burlington cemetery and returned home to be near his grieving mother. After three years, the Goulds relinquished ownership of the cemetery to the citizens of Niwot so that others in the community could be buried there as well.

Native vegetation blankets the grounds of the Niwot cemetery. Attempts to dig a well failed, so folks hauled water to the flowers and shrubs they had planted on family plots. *Courtesy of the author.*

For years, there was little supervision of the burial grounds, and it wasn't until Evan buried his wife in the old cemetery that he began to notice its run-down appearance. He enlisted the help of the Longmont VFW in maintaining the grounds but observed that their clean-up days included drinking beer while they worked. Local families disapproved and took the necessary steps to form a cemetery association. Since that time, maintenance of the grounds has been overseen by families whose ancestors are buried there.

The cemetery has retained its "pioneer" status over the years because most of its burials have been descendants of early settlers. It is said, however, that plots in the northeast corner were never sold because of unmarked graves dug in the dark of night by local indigent families.

Existing grave markers range from primitive wooden crosses to carved granite monuments. Some plots are outlined by large rocks or bricks, while others have only simple footstones to indicate boundaries. Other graves are more difficult to locate because their markers have disappeared or rotted away.

Vandals desecrated the cemetery in 1991, stealing the gates and overturning or breaking several gravestones. But the community responded by raising $1,000 to repair the damage. Today, the Niwot cemetery appears tidy and well cared for. It lies along quiet Nimbus Road and, at least for now, remains surrounded by pristine farmland.

ALL ABOARD

Niwot was a railroad town, platted soon after the Colorado Central Railroad tracks were laid between Boulder and Longmont. Its original business district stood along Hinman Street behind the depot west of the tracks. After 1900, new commercial buildings were built along Second Avenue, east of the tracks.

Although many of the twentieth-century buildings remain standing today, all of them west of the tracks are gone—including the depot. In its heyday, the railroad station was the heart and soul of the town, where farm products were loaded into boxcars headed to market and youngsters boarded the train to attend high school in Boulder or Longmont. It was the place where mail was delivered twice a day, cattle were loaded into cattle cars bound for distant stockyards and crates of baby chicks arrived every spring.

Freight, milk cans, egg crates and luggage were stacked on platform wagons waiting to be loaded onto the next train. Mailbags were readied for delivery to Longmont or Boulder, and occasionally someone dropped by with an urgent message for agent/telegrapher Will T. Wilson to dispatch. Joe Archuleta was always on hand to assist Will's wife, Delia, with platform chores. There was a mail hook beside the track where outgoing mailbags could be snagged by north- and southbound freight trains. Incoming bags were tossed onto the platform as the trains rolled slowly by. Only occasionally did they miss their mark and land farther down the track.

Newton Spangler was the station agent when the depot closed in 1932. Years later, the building was cut in half, leaving only the freight portion intact. At that point, Niwot was considered a *flag stop*, where trains were flagged down only if an unscheduled passenger wanted to board or if there were more mailbags than could be hung from the mail hook.

"Fellowship between railroad people hangs on for years," Newt's son Don Spangler observed. "When trains came through at night, they would toot at the railroad crossing, and Dad would leap out of bed to flash his porch light at the crew. He knew those engineers by their whistle."

John Dodd photographed the Niwot depot from atop the flour mill elevator across the street. From the boxcars parked behind the depot to the telegraph line along the tracks and the sugar beet ramp in the distance, this picture illustrates the importance of the railroad to commerce in town. *Courtesy of Niwot Historical Society.*

BUILDING BLOCKS

"There is big profit in making concrete building blocks," claimed the headline in the 1908 Sears, Roebuck & Company catalogue. According to a three-page spread devoted to their Wizard Concrete Building Block Machine, this emerging business opportunity was the answer for any entrepreneur or individual property owner looking for a cheaper and fire-resistant building product for his home, outbuilding or storefront.

The Wizard cost $42.50 and was capable of molding two eight- by eight-by sixteen-inch blocks at a time. It was hand-operated, and in order to stress its simplicity, Sears claimed that an individual could easily make blocks during his spare time "or on a rainy day."

Buyers were offered a choice of fourteen block surfaces including plain, tooled or cobblestone. The more decorative versions incorporated rope or scroll designs. Perhaps the most common texture, however, was the standard rock face, a style still found locally on some early buildings. With a texture that resembles quarried stone, Niwot's Wise Buys Antiques building at 198 Second Avenue is a classic example.

Harmon S. Palmer designed the first concrete block machine in 1890, with removable cores and adjustable sides. After ten years of experimenting, he obtained a patent and is credited with developing the first commercial process for manufacturing concrete blocks in the United States.

Block machines could weigh as much as five hundred pounds, but they were considered portable and could be moved to any construction site. This saved builders the cost of shipping and lessened the possibility of breakage in handling.

In a 1993 interview, Amy Sherman told of her father, Charles Sherman, making blocks in Niwot in the early 1900s. At that early date, in 1907, it is possible that he was helping builder John Nelson construct the Niwot Mercantile, which today is the home of Wise Buys Antiques.

Although Sears described its block machines as the means to a profitable business, Skip Hicks, who lives north of Hygiene, says that most folks just used them for their own projects. The only local commercial block business he could recall belonged to Lou Newsum, who produced concrete blocks at the old Hygiene elevator years ago.

Skip has a block machine that he hasn't used for years. Unlike the Sears Wizard, however, his makes only one block at a time. "It's a horrible job," he explained. "If you wanted to work really, really hard, you could probably make maybe fifteen blocks in a day." Skip's blocks weighed fifty to sixty pounds each, and although difficult to handle, they were a far cry from Harmon Palmer's eight- by ten- by thirty-inch prototypes. Those required a small crane to set in place.

From Humble Beginnings

If you were to ask Niwot Elementary School students today how old their school building is, many probably couldn't tell you. To most of them, the building "has always been there." But historically, it is the fifth schoolhouse in a span of 141 years to be called a Niwot school.

According to Doyle Hornbaker, former editor of the *Niwot Tribune*, the first schoolhouse in the Left Hand Valley was a small log structure built west of the cemetery. Only a pencil sketch, drawn from memory by Jerome Gould, remains as proof of its existence. It dated from about 1863, when the first nine Boulder County school districts were established. The structure wasn't fancy—just one room with tiny windows and a chimney at one end for the potbelly stove.

As the only school district serving the entire Left Hand Valley, the attendance area for District #7 was huge, stretching from Nelson Road south to Lookout Road and from Highway 287 west to the foothills. It wasn't long before escalating enrollment forced the county school superintendent to split the Niwot district in two, creating the Bader District for students living closer to the foothills.

At about the same time that the town of Niwot and the railroad appeared in the Left Hand Valley, a second schoolhouse was built at Eighty-first Street and Oxford Road. With lap siding, a shingled roof and a potbelly stove, it resembled almost every other schoolhouse of that period. There were thirty-five students enrolled and one teacher, whose take-home pay was forty-seven dollars a month.

In 1902, a larger schoolhouse was built on Niwot Road at Franklin Street. Called Willowdale School by the locals, it too was soon outgrown and replaced with a fourth schoolhouse just northwest of town. This two-story brick structure was considerably larger than its predecessors and remained occupied from 1910 until 1967. Unfortunately, it stood where the westbound lane of a proposed highway between Boulder and Longmont was soon to be built. It remained empty until 1972, when it was sold for $1,800 to the Colorado State Department of Highways, which demolished it.

News of the new highway project reached Niwot in the late 1950s, allowing ample time to build a fifth elementary school east of town. This time, the

These 1913 eighth graders were the first class to graduate from the new Niwot Elementary School. Built only three years earlier, it still lacked landscaping and playground equipment. *Courtesy of Niwot Historical Society.*

district anticipated future growth with an even larger facility. Today, Niwot Elementary School has a capacity of six hundred students, although current enrollment stands at five hundred.

The Willowdale schoolhouse remains standing as a reminder of Niwot's early days. It harkens back to a time when children walked to school, brought their lunches from home, wrote their lessons on slate tablets and carved their names on their desks.

A Short Commute

Ask teachers at today's Niwot elementary school how far they drive to work each day, and their answers will likely range from five to ten miles. A century ago, this was not the case.

School records dating back to 1900 show that some of Niwot's teachers were local residents who probably walked to their jobs. Those who lived in Boulder or Longmont could easily commute by train or stay with local families during the week. It was common practice for a family with several children enrolled in class to provide room and board for the schoolmarm if she lived far from town.

District #7 encompassed much of the Left Hand Valley. One of its first teachers was Estelle Edwards. The thirty-two children in her tiny one-room schoolhouse west of Niwot spanned grades one through eight and probably represented only a fraction of the eligible children in the district. The 1870 census indicated that there were almost four thousand school-aged children in Boulder County, but fewer than half were actually enrolled in school. The county spent $3.53 per month to educate those who did attend at that time. Estelle received $47.00 a month for the six-month school term.

In 1898, before school laws required teachers to be certified, Boulder County listed sixteen teachers under the age of eighteen. Luella Henry was thirty, however, when she taught at Niwot's Willowdale School in 1907. She was one of six children born to Nimrod Henry, a local farmer, banker and businessman. Along with her mother and sisters, Luella belonged to the local chapters of the Rebekahs, Royal Neighbors and Ladies Aid Society. Remaining single, she lived with her parents for many years.

Luella Henry, on the right, was just one of four young teachers when she taught at an unidentified school in Wyoming. *Courtesy of Niwot Historical Society.*

Amy Stockley, another local girl, was hired by District #7 in 1909, at a salary of forty-five dollars per month. This was 10 percent less than her male counterparts were earning. Amy was the second daughter of Niwot's postmaster, Julia Stockley. Like Luella, she never married.

Idell McKee taught in Niwot from 1921 to 1923. By this time, the district had built a new schoolhouse northwest of town and turned the one on Niwot Road into a teacherage. During her brief teaching career, Idell lived in the teacherage and walked the short distance to her job. Because she was forbidden to marry during the term of her contract, Idell retired before marrying Charles Kneale, who farmed just east of town.

For the record, teaching salaries by the 1920s had skyrocketed to seventy-five dollars per month, with equal pay for both men and women.

Before the Snow Flies

What have you done to prepare for winter this year? For most of us, such arrangements are limited to putting up storm windows, dragging out the snow tires and airing out our winter clothing. A century ago, however, preparations were much different.

During October, farmers were digging sugar beets, the last crop to be harvested before the ground froze. Folks in Niwot observed a steady line of horse-drawn wagons slowly moving down Second Avenue toward the beet ramp at the west end of Third Avenue. There, an empty Great Western Sugar Company boxcar stood on a sidetrack with a narrow ramp looming above it. The line of wagons inched toward the ramp as each farmer drove his team to the top and tipped the wagon to release the beets into a waiting boxcar below. When the car was full, it was hauled to the sugar refinery in Longmont, and an empty beet car took its place.

After crops were in, farmers had time to repair their machinery. George Atkinson's blacksmith shop was a busy place in the fall. Farm implements were crowded into the empty lot next door, waiting their turn to be welded, sharpened or otherwise made ready for another growing season.

At home, families were busy preserving the last of the season's harvest for the winter months. Root cellars were common, and by wintertime, they were stocked with root crops and crocks of preserved meats. Silvia Manchester recalled how her mother "fried down" pork to be placed in crocks and covered with freshly rendered lard. Delores Bailey described retrieving meat during the winter by reaching into the lard to pull out

The Niwot beet ramp was built in 1916 and replaced the dump north of town where sugar beets were piled onto the ground beside a railroad sidetrack. When an empty Great Western Sugar Company boxcar was brought in, the beets were tossed by pitchfork into it. It was then hauled to the sugar factory in Longmont. *Courtesy of Niwot Historical Society.*

sausages for a family meal. Others preferred baking their meat and then cold-packing it in jars.

Ara Kossler remembered the root cellar behind their ranch house on Flagstaff Mountain. "In the back," she said, "there were real deep shelves that held five rows of quart bottles. In the center of the cellar floor stood a fifty-gallon barrel of sauerkraut."

Fruit crops were plentiful along the Front Range in the 1880s, and early photographs reveal acres of orchards and vineyards north of Boulder, which belonged to Joseph Wolff. He often hired women and children to harvest his vast fields of strawberries. Much of this fresh produce was purchased by housewives to be preserved for the winter as jellies, jams and whole fruit.

Ernest Pease recalled Thanksgiving dinners with luscious side dishes of home-canned tomatoes, watermelon pickles, jellies and plum butter. When he studied mythology in later years and read of the "ambrosia and nectar favored of the gods," he doubted that their food could equal the delicacies his mother had prepared for her family so many years before.

ADDRESS UNKNOWN

In this age of global positioning and MapQuest, it is hard to imagine the primitive methods used to locate addresses in the late 1800s.

The first roads in Boulder County were mainly dirt paths along section lines, and most were unnamed. As settlement continued, farmers began pressuring the county commissioners to improve them. The dirt road extending east from Boulder, for instance, was known locally as Valley Road. But in 1891, fourteen adjoining landowners successfully petitioned the commissioners to officially change its name to Arapahoe Avenue. (The misspelling of Arapaho was never corrected and still appears on all of its street signs).

Porter Hinman and Ambrose Murray named all of Niwot's streets when they submitted the town plat in 1875. But because residents received their mail at the local post office, neither town nor rural residences were numbered.

How would *you* have located someone's home if you didn't know his or her address or phone number? All you had to do was ask. The reply went something like this: "He lives over by the beet dump" or "It's that farmhouse down past the mill" or "Turn right at the Johnson barn."

In the late 1800s, Boulder city directories were introduced, with separate sections for each of the smaller communities in the county. No street addresses were given, but listed beside every individual's name was his occupation. The Niwot section included the following: Val Brown, surfacing gang foreman for UPD&G Railway, and William Hornbaker, farmer and justice of the peace.

Directories published after 1900 began to include wives' names as well: William Arbuthnot (Clara), farmer; Henry Null (Fannie), shoe repair.

When Longmont granted Mountain States Telephone and Telegraph Company a franchise in 1899, phone directories were distributed, but without street addresses. Browsing through the circa 1910 phone book archived at the Longmont Museum, one finds that only twenty-three Niwot businesses and residential phone numbers were listed. Among them were:

Blue 672 Nimrod Henry—rancher—near Niwot
Blue 321 A. T. Jones—horseman—near Niwot
White 94 Niwot State Bank—Niwot

Modern communication had come a long way by this time, but folks still didn't have street addresses. If they had phones, however, a Mountain States

Telephone operator could connect parties with anyone they wished to call. As the company stated in the back of its early phone books, "The savings in car fare alone will more than pay for a Bell telephone in the home."

NIMROD HENRY

Nimrod Henry, or "Nim," as he preferred to be called, was among hundreds of homesteaders who headed west after the Civil War. He was only eighteen when he and his father planned to drive a flock of sheep to Colorado Territory to sell in the gold camps. The trip was cancelled, however, when a neighbor offered them top dollar for the entire flock.

Disappointed, yet still dreaming of the frontier, Nimrod left home in 1865 and began his long walk from Mahaska County, Iowa, to the Rocky Mountains. He worked briefly at odd jobs around Denver, including employment as a farmhand on what is now Capitol Hill. Feeling the need to put down roots, however, he headed north out of Denver in 1870 to find suitable farmland. He found it in the Left Hand Valley, north of Boulder, and staked his claim along Dry Creek. After building a house on today's Monarch Road, he asked his childhood sweetheart, Melissa Linson, to come west to marry him. They were wed in Central City in 1873.

Having been stricken with polio in childhood, Melissa walked by bracing one hand on her knee. Soon after the birth of their third child, she was permanently crippled when a wagon wheel struck her knee. Being as determined as her husband, however, she bore him six children and became known as the best sidesaddle rider in the valley.

Nimrod had a keen business sense, and drawing on his farming experience, he helped to establish several of Niwot's agricultural enterprises. He served as vice-president of the Niwot Alfalfa Milling Company and became president of the Niwot Creamery. His signature even appears on the petition requesting establishment of the Niwot post office in 1874. As one of the organizers of the Niwot State Bank, he served for years as its president. And as the father of six children, he spent many years as a member of the School District #7 school board.

Nim loved to argue politics and was known to turn on his heel and walk away from anyone with whom he disagreed. He was always first in line on election day, when the polls opened at the grange hall west of the tracks. He couldn't wait to circle the word "Democrat" at the top of his ballot. This gesture alone indicated his vote on all the candidates.

A bit older but still standing erect, Nimrod posed with his grandson, Paul Henry, who as a boy probably milked the cows for his grandfather's daily ration of fresh milk. *Courtesy of Betty Clifford.*

Idell Leinweber vividly remembers the elderly Nimrod striding through town every morning toward his son Horace's farm on Seventy-ninth Street to get his daily bucket of fresh milk. Don Spangler, too, recalls watching him follow the tracks on his daily milk run. "You could almost set your watch by him," he chuckled.

Nimrod Henry died in 1940 at the age of ninety-two. Years later, Tony DiSanto reflected on this remarkable man: "I can hardly believe I used to talk with somebody that fought in the Civil War."

The Outlaw Bill Dubois

Although he committed numerous crimes over the years, it was the murder of Ed Kinney that sent young William "Bill" Dubois running for his life.

Early accounts of Bill's activities in the St. Vrain Valley gave no hint of the profound turn his life would eventually take. The Dubois family had come to Colorado Territory in about 1860, settling near the mouth of Left Hand Canyon. Bill was only twenty-one years old, but he seemed well on his way to a productive life. The fact that his name appeared on the incorporation papers for the nearby town of Altona suggests that he was involved in civic affairs at an early age.

Shortly thereafter, he laid claim to land east of Burlington, a small community south of today's Longmont. There, he built a log cabin and made plans to establish a meat market.

Gradually, folks around Burlington began noticing that Bill was keeping company with questionable characters like Jack Watkins, who often bragged that he had once killed a man "just for the fun of it."

On the day after Christmas 1869, Dubois and three of his friends were arrested for holding up and wounding the driver of a stagecoach carrying passengers and mail. Among the witnesses called to testify at his trial was Ed Kinney, the assistant Burlington postmaster. Although Kinney chose not to testify (claiming that he had no knowledge of the event), he was already a marked man. While awaiting trial, the suspects had compiled a list of those they thought were responsible for their arrest, and Kinney was among them. Trial testimony failed to produce conclusive evidence against the young men, so they were released.

Soon afterward, however, each man on the list received a threatening note demanding $300 to reimburse the defendants for their trouble and expense. Dubois had sold the mortgage on his claim east of Burlington to pay court costs and was trying to recoup his losses. None of the men responded, nor did they give much thought to the payment deadline of March 1, 1870. But as the deadline approached, Dubois took desperate measures that touched off a deadly chain of events.

On February 22, Kinney enlisted John H. Wells to drive with him to the Larimer County line to retrieve a wayward colt. On their return, Kinney was seated in the back of the wagon, legs dangling over the edge, leading the colt by its halter. As the men approached Burlington, they were suddenly confronted by Dubois, who angrily demanded his $300.

According to Wells's account of the incident, both men rebuffed him. Dubois drew his revolver and shot twice at Kinney. The wagon team lurched forward, and the startled colt jumped back, pulling Kinney out of the wagon. Dubois continued to fire at him as he fell dead by the side of the road. He then sped off at a full gallop toward the safety of his father's cabin on Left Hand Creek, while Wells continued on to Burlington with equal haste.

A local posse (including Sylvanus Budd and Jerome Gould of Niwot) was quickly formed, and within hours, the Dubois family cabin was surrounded. Bill escaped on horseback, however, and headed for Left Hand Canyon less than a mile away. But he had been wounded during the fracas and emerged from the canyon the following morning bleeding and in pain. Determined not to be taken alive, he rode toward the waiting posse, his rifle pointed straight ahead. Within minutes, he was dead.

His body was returned to Burlington, where it was dumped in the street before a relieved crowd. Charley Baker, a local carpenter and member of the posse, prepared the body for burial in a homemade coffin. Dubois was then returned to the family homestead and placed beside the grave of his mother and a younger sister.

According to B.L. Boyle's written account of the tragedy, Bill's brother later rode into Burlington, paid the amount due for the coffin and left without comment.

Part III

EARLY NIWOT BUSINESSES

SMALL CATTLE OPERATIONS

Most farmers in the Left Hand Valley raised a variety of livestock both for their own use and for market—dairy herds, poultry, hogs and a few head of cattle. The cattle were driven to summer pasture each spring, then home again in the fall. Because they intermingled with other herds, a means of permanent identification was essential.

The Spaniards brought branding irons from Europe to the New World, and the practice of branding cattle became an integral part of ranching in the American Southwest. In 1899, Colorado established legislation governing the registration of all brands in the state. The first brand book was published in 1900. These were updated every ten years until 1962, when they began printing updates every five years.

The thirty-six thousand brands currently on record in Colorado include those registered for cattle, horses, mules, burros, donkeys and any other livestock that change ownership or are transported more than seventy-five miles within the state. Colorado still employs brand inspectors to verify ownership at the time of the sale or transporting of livestock.

Today, more than 347 brands are registered in Boulder County alone—some dating back to the late 1860s. Scattered among them are familiar pioneer names like Gould, Cushman, Knaus and Kneale from Niwot. Thomas Kneale came to America from the Isle of Man with his brother Charles in the 1870s. They were followed soon after by their mother and a third brother, Philip. For several years, the three brothers operated a thriving sawmill operation in

The Kneale farmhouse still stands on Niwot Road, east of Eighty-third Street. Thomas and his wife, Georgiana, are standing at the left. *Courtesy of Idell Kneale Leinweber.*

Eldorado Canyon, south of Boulder. Thomas left the business in about 1888, however, to claim a 240-acre homestead on Niwot Road, just east of Eighty-third Street. There he maintained a large herd of cattle.

After Thomas passed away, his son Albert continued to raise cattle and herded them to summer pasture in St. Vrain Canyon each spring. After they were driven back to the farm in the fall, all the summer calves were branded with the family brand: Cross Bar Bell.

Albert's daughter, Idell (Leinweber), helped to drive the cattle down Niwot Road to the loading pens behind the Niwot depot each fall. From there, they were shipped to the Union Stockyards in Denver. Although still too young to drive legally, Idell followed behind the herd in the family truck to bring the crew home once the cattle were in the corrals. She still has the family branding iron.

The Ultimate Wish Book

Mabel Andre Thomas fondly recalled taking violin lessons as a child from the local baker in Louisville. Her family had purchased the instrument from a Sears or Montgomery Ward catalogue—she couldn't remember which.

"They paid five or ten dollars for it," she said. "It proved to be a valuable violin. I was offered $100 for it years later."

When John Darby was the star pitcher for the Armstrong School north of Longmont in the 1920s, he preferred baseballs purchased through the Montgomery Ward catalogue "because they came with a twenty-seven-inning guarantee."

Indeed, Wards' guarantee policy was its key to gaining the respect and trust of rural families in an age when wholesale merchandising *direct to the consumer* was a totally new concept. Families eagerly anticipated the arrival of each new catalogue, which was delivered several times a year. It provided a reliable source of both useful and frivolous products for every member of the household.

When Aaron Montgomery Ward issued his first mail-order catalogue in 1872, it was only a one-page list of 162 items. So innovative was its marketing concept, however, that within three years it had grown to a seventy-two-page booklet describing over two thousand products. His original motto, "Satisfaction or Your Money Back," appeared inside the front cover.

Although the 1875 catalogue measured only three by five inches, it was filled with items needed for running a household or a farming operation: from yard goods and sewing machines to bed springs and farm wagons. By this time, the company had been declared the official supply house for the Patrons of Husbandry, better known as the Grange, and testimonials from satisfied grangers filled several pages.

Montgomery Ward & Company reigned as the nation's premier mail-order house until the late 1880s, when Richard W. Sears, a watch salesman, and Alvah C. Roebuck, a watch repairman, entered the market. Their first catalogue appeared in 1887 but was confined to watches, jewelry and silverware. They quickly diversified, however, and by the 1890s, the most popular items sold through their thirty-two-page catalogue were sewing machines, bicycles and cream separators. Prices for sewing machines varied from twenty to thirty dollars, and a good bicycle could be purchased for thirty-five dollars plus shipping. The Peerless cream separator came in various models, depending on the customer's needs. They could process milk from three or four cows or from a herd as large as thirty-six. All models were available at 40 percent below the factory price.

Grocery items were introduced to the Sears catalogue in 1896, and rural families could order items from as far away as Europe and the Orient. All manner of canned goods, flour, spices, beauty aids, cigars and homeopathic remedies were now available by mail.

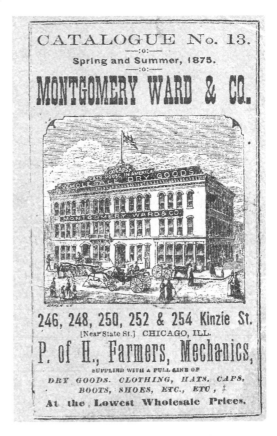

The 1875 Wards catalogue proudly described itself as the "Cheapest Cash House in America." Grange members could order official officers' regalia, including a regulation wool top hat for $1.25, and ladies full-length cotton aprons and sashes, bound in crimson braid.

Both Sears and Wards considered rural Americans their primary mail-order target customers. But when Wards opened its first retail store in 1926, it found itself competing with department stores that were already supplying the needs of an urbanized America. Business further declined in 1985, when it discontinued its catalogue. Realizing its mistake, it attempted to resurrect the catalogue in 1991, but it was too late. In 2000, 128 years after its inception, Montgomery Ward & Company filed for bankruptcy.

Prairie Sentinels

Here in the St. Vrain Valley, silos are one of the most enduring reminders of our agricultural past. Seemingly indestructible, they don't decay or sag with age the way barns do. Built to withstand wind, weather and moisture, they have evolved from the concrete-stave silos of the late 1890s to the metal and fiberglass giants seen today. Yet with the rapid urbanization of Boulder County, most remaining silos have outlived their usefulness and are gradually disappearing from the landscape.

If you look closely, you'll discover that not all silos are alike. The earliest ones in Boulder County were made of two-inch boards stacked horizontally, much like a rectangular granary. Wood is subject to rot, of course, and air trapped in the corners allows silage to decay. Because of this, few wooden silos remain. Stuart Anderson, however, still maintains the wooden octagonal silo built by his grandfather, Emil Anderson, in 1920. Empty now and leaning just a bit, it still stands on the family homestead.

The first poured concrete silo in Boulder County dates from 1907, when Nels Anderson brought two sixteen-foot-diameter forms with him from Minnesota. Using this new equipment, he built two silos to store silage for his dairy herd west of Niwot. Nels paid his son Ted ten cents a bushel to gather rocks for the concrete mix. After the first layer of concrete had hardened, subsequent layers were poured until the desired height was reached. Both Anderson silos are still standing at 5939 Niwot Road.

"My dad built a concrete silo like that in 1921," Wayne Arbuthnot recalled. "They hauled the sand from a gulch on Table Mountain and screened it for dirt. They didn't have concrete mixers, [so they used] a mixing box."

Nels Anderson donated the sixteen-foot-diameter forms used to construct his two concrete silos to the state agricultural college (now Colorado State University) in Fort Collins. *Courtesy of the author.*

Stave silos are still fairly common throughout the West. They were constructed of tongue-and-groove concrete blocks stacked alternately, much like a circular brick wall. At eight- to fifteen-inch intervals, steel strapping hoops were tightened around the exterior to prevent leakage. Although their design dates from the 1890s, it wasn't until about 1914 that stave silos appeared in Boulder County. That's when the Colorado Cement Stave Silo Company of Longmont began marketing their Playford model. The sales brochure described them as "scientifically correct," with steel reinforcements so exactly balanced that the walls would never crack. In addition, the interior was treated with a waterproof coating to make it impervious to the acid juices of the ensilage.

Danish immigrant Carl Carlson bought a Playford silo in 1923. Still standing at 10050 Plateau Road, it measures almost fifty-five feet tall, as compared to a standard silo, which stands less than forty-five-feet in height. Because it is thought to be the tallest silo in Boulder County, the county commissioners landmarked the Carlson silo in 1999.

The next time you drive through the countryside, slow down at the next silo and take a closer look.

THE VILLAGE SMITHY

After Niwot was founded as a railroad shipping point for local farm products, it began to take on the features of many western farming communities. Most of its early businesses provided services needed by farmers in the area: dry goods and grocery stores, implement dealers, blacksmith shops, feed mills and a local bank.

Some merchants established businesses and then moved on. Others prospered and became permanent fixtures in the community. The Atkinson family, for instance, remained tied to Niwot from 1923 until the 1980s, during which time George Atkinson and his son Walter repaired farm implements for two generations of local farmers.

When George arrived in Niwot in 1923, he assumed the reins of his predecessor, William Sutton, who had died tragically the previous year. Doyle Jones still remembers that fateful day in 1922 when he left two of his road-crew horses with Sutton to be shod. Sutton told Jones to leave the team and return for them later in the day. Sometime during his absence, one of the horses kicked Sutton in the head, killing him instantly. Although both George and Walter Atkinson were expert welders and skilled craftsmen, this may explain why both refused to ever shoe horses.

There had been other blacksmiths before Atkinson came to town. Jim Hood arrived in the late 1800s and set up shop in the original business district west of the railroad tracks. At about the same time, the 1896 county business directory listed John Nelson as a local farrier and wagon maker. Frank Polzin set up his blacksmith shop in 1916, in the 400 block of Franklin Street, but stayed only a few years before moving his family to Valmont.

In addition to sharpening sickle blades and repairing or replacing broken machine parts, both George and Walter Atkinson forged branding irons for local cattlemen. They field-tested them by burning the brands into the large double doors of their blacksmith shop. In the wintertime, when fieldwork was finished, George fashioned specialized truck beds with side-dump chains for hauling sugar beets up the sugar beet ramp and dumping the contents into boxcars below. Locals speculate that some of them are probably still around in farmyards today.

When George retired after World War II, he turned the business over to his son Walter, who continued operating it until his death in about 1980. Glowing testimonials are still given by those who knew them. Don Spangler, who learned to weld by observing George at work, remarked, "George didn't talk very much. [But] he talked more after a few sips of wine than he did

George Atkinson carried tobacco products and fishing tackle in the back of his blacksmith shop on Second Avenue. *Courtesy of Niwot Historical Society.*

before. He could fix anything that broke," Don continued. "He could wire weld with an acetylene torch and a piece of baling wire and make anything look like new."

WHO WAS REVEREND TAYLOR?

Rev Taylor's restaurant on Second Avenue was a popular Niwot eating destination from 1985 until 2000. People on foot and on bicycles lined up every weekend morning as they waited to be seated. Most of them still remember the name but wonder, "Who was Rev Taylor?"

William E. Taylor was a respected Niwot grocer in the early 1900s. He was born in 1870 and moved as a child to Niwot in 1880. As a young man, he became an ordained United Brethren minister and preached briefly at the Niwot United Brethren Church at 304 Franklin Street; later, he preached in the meeting room he built above his grocery store on Second Avenue. After his marriage, William and his wife, Ada, moved to a house just east of today's Niwot Feed Store on Second Avenue, where they raised their family.

Taylor opened his first grocery store in 1912, on the first floor of Nelson Hall at the corner of Second Avenue and Franklin Street. John Nelson had completed the building only a few years before. When Taylor's Niwot Bee outgrew the space in Nelson Hall, he built his own store at the west end of the block. It included a second-floor meeting room where he continued to preach whenever he could get enough worshippers together. His new grocery store was called the White House.

As a young man, Evan Gould hauled foundation rock for its construction. He described William Taylor as a large, balding man, strong enough to haul sides of beef from the Niwot depot to a walk-in cooler at the back of his store. Taylor was a respected butcher and was often hired to supply meat and produce to the many mobile cook wagons that operated during threshing season. If a depot platform wagon wasn't available when the train arrived, Taylor carried the beef on his back to the cooler. In the wintertime, he also borrowed the wagon to haul block ice harvested from Dodd Lake to his cooler.

Taylor was widowed by the time he retired in 1934. He filled his days by working part time on Doyle and Luvesta Jones's chicken farm on Neva Road. The Joneses couldn't afford to pay him, but they always fed him dinner and sent him home with fresh eggs.

Recalling stories told by his grandfather Henry Hornbaker, Don Spangler described Reverend Taylor as rather eccentric. He related the time in the 1920s

The interior of the White House grocery store was spotless, and Taylor was never without his butcher's apron when he was working. *Courtesy of Niwot Historical Society.*

when Taylor took the night train home from an appointment in Denver. The train didn't stop in Niwot at night, and Taylor couldn't convince the engineer to let him off at the depot. "He was a little perturbed," Don said, "because he'd have to go all the way to Longmont and walk home late at night." So Taylor waited until the train slowed to fifteen miles an hour on the curve north of town, opened the window and jumped out. After a passenger reported, "Some guy fell out of the window," the railroad section crew was sent to search in the dark for "the suicide." Of course, they came up empty-handed.

PIONEER NEWSPAPERS

The *Left Hand Valley Courier* is one of the latest in an impressive list of newspapers published in Boulder County over the past 131 years. In that time period, more than 110 daily, weekly and monthly papers have come and gone. On their mastheads were popular names like the *Tribune*, *Post*, *Times*, *Pioneer*, *Sentinel* and *Free Press*. Some of them survived mergers, buyouts and name changes to remain viable for years. Others failed after only one edition. Longmont's *Inter-Ocean* newspaper lasted two years before merging with the *Rocky Mountain Eagle* in 1875 to become the *Boulder Bee*.

As newspapers flourished or floundered, printing presses were passed from town to town, purchased by men eager to influence settlement along the Front Range. In 1867, Boulder actually stole the presses from Valmont, its neighbor to the east. Historical accounts of the deed vary, but whatever the version, Valmont came up empty-handed.

These two communities were in fierce competition to become the county seat, and Valmont appeared to have the edge. It had established the county's first newspaper, the *Valmont Bulletin*. Whether editor and co-owner Daniel Scouten actually knew of the caper or was an unwitting victim is unknown, but after the presses were moved to Boulder in the dead of night, Scouten emerged on its first payroll.

The other co-owner of the now voiceless *Bulletin* was Dr. Henley Allen, one of Valmont's founders. When his pilfered presses began printing the *Boulder Valley News* the following month, Allen submitted this poem to its editor:

> *Our press is gone and we are lost,*
> *While some have got the blues.*
> *We want it back at any cost,*
> *The Boulder Valley News.*

The plethora of newspapers during Boulder County's early years is understandable. The isolation experienced by early settlers was somewhat assuaged by reading local and national news reports. If one newspaper was informative, subscribing to several papers was even better. When the descendants of Canfield's Oliver Ellsworth Wise disposed of his old papers a few years ago, they found subscriptions to more than seven newspapers dating from the 1870s and 1880s. As both a businessman and a farmer, Wise had surrounded himself with labor news, stockmen journals and mining newspapers, as well as subscriptions to several local publications.

Old newspapers today are a valuable source of information to researchers, as well as those simply seeking a glimpse into the past. Browsing through their ads, flowery obituaries and social columns is a great way to learn more about Boulder County's history.

When the Colorado Newspaper Project was undertaken in 1987, the Colorado Historical Society began searching for old issues from all corners of the state. With a grant from the National Endowment for the Humanities, they copied fifteen hundred Colorado newspaper titles onto twenty-three hundred miles of microfilm. Their search yielded many surprises, including the discovery of unknown newspapers, as well as proof that some papers had been in print longer than previously documented.

NIWOT'S GROCERY LIST

The historic plaque on Chris Finger's Pianos building reads, "Esgar Mercantile—built 1911." Little was known about Frank Esgar until his granddaughter, Debi Christensen of Nederland, contacted the Niwot Historical Society about her family and donated several photos to its collection.

Frank Traver Esgar was born in Illinois in 1848, the son of Welch immigrants. Unmarried and in his forties, he finally left Illinois and headed west. "He came to Boulder, Colorado around 1890–1900," Debi explained. There he co-owned a grocery store on North Broadway. After their marriage in 1906, Frank and Eleanor Tomlin Esgar left Boulder and moved to a farm northeast of town to raise their family. They were gradually inching their way toward Niwot.

Frank must have missed the grocery business because in about 1920, he and his family left the farm and moved into Niwot. There he opened a general store on the corner of Murray Street and Second Avenue. Next door was Reverend Taylor's White House Grocery and Meat Market, which soon

Eleanor Tomlin was considerably younger than Frank Esgar when they married in 1906. Shortly after their marriage, they moved from Boulder to a farm northeast of town. *Courtesy of Debra Christensen.*

became his closest competitor. "He had some overlapping merchandise in the mercantile that he ran," Debi said.

The family moved into a bungalow at 520 Murray Street, just three blocks north of his store. Both Marjorie and Frank Jr. enrolled in the Niwot Elementary School, which was conveniently located directly across the tracks from their home. Today, the Diagonal Highway bisects what would have been the children's direct route to school.

One of the few published news items about Frank Esgar appeared in a 1925 issue of the *Niwot Tribune*. He was quoted by the reporter as saying, "Our meat supply has become so heavy, the ice box dropped through the floor. John Young is now engaged in repairing the floor.

Esgar Mercantile, along with other businesses in town, prospered until the stock market crash of 1929. When the Niwot State Bank folded in 1931, faithful customers moved their savings to Longmont and began doing their marketing there as well. The Esgars were forced to close their store and return to Boulder.

Today, a piano store occupies Esgar's mercantile building. Frank, Eleanor and their two children are now deceased, and all that validates their time here is the historic plaque by the front door of Chris Finger Pianos.

THE VERSATILE TIN LIZZIE

Transportation in the Left Hand Valley began to change in the early 1900s. While farms were still being cultivated with horse-drawn equipment, the farmers themselves were converting to automobiles. The most popular "first family car" in the Niwot area was the Model T Ford because of its $500 price tag and its versatility. Although originally designed to transport passengers from place to place, Model Ts were adapted to many other uses. For farmers, their twenty-horsepower engines easily surpassed draft teams in pulling hay rakes and plows through the fields. As a substitute for stationary steam engines, they could also power hay balers, log splitters and silage cutters.

For vacationing families, camping accessories such as canvas tents and storage trunks conveniently retrofitted onto running boards and rooftops. In the days before roadside motels, the freedom to travel in comfort became all the rage. Niwot's Lee Forsythe used his Model T coupe to haul fellow dance band members and their instruments to gigs all over the county. Clarence Conilogue replaced his horse-drawn mail wagon with a Model T in 1916. And John Dodd recalled selling his family's dilapidated Tin Lizzie in the

1920s to a young man "who stripped it of its body for a racing unit, and [threw] the body onto the banks of Dry Creek—a stark reminder of its better days as we drove by."

As versatile as these early cars were, however, they still needed fuel. Some merchants along Second Avenue installed hand-operated gas pumps in front of their establishments. Pumps stood in front of today's Curves and Wise Buys Antiques.

Recently, another early gas station location was revealed. Now a residence, it still stands at the corner of Seventy-third Street and Niwot Road. In the early 1920s, it was owned and operated by the Alvah Dodd family. Alvah's son John, mentioned earlier, wrote about the gas station in his memoirs:

> *As I recall, there were two filling stations in downtown Niwot, not counting the Buchert station across the railroad tracks. Even though the demand, as we found out, for another station was not justified, Father had in mind starting one on the [Dodd Lake] corner. Could it have been to make a job for me? I wonder! Anyway, I spent a lot of time there selling gas, oil, sweet corn, pop, cigarettes (Father never did approve of them), and free information.*

The Polzin brothers' versatile Model T became sleeping quarters when equipped with a canvas tarp attached to its roof. *Courtesy of Lois Polzin McGinty.*

When business declined, the pumps were retired. "As a last resort," John wrote, "a nice repair shop was added and rented to a young man and his brother-in-law, who owned a team of horses for hire." When business picked up again, the old family bunkhouse was moved across the road for living quarters behind the shop.

After its conversion to a home, John's brother Hugh and his family moved in. In the 1940s, a two-bedroom addition was attached to the west side, and the home was complete. To Nancy Dodd Hindman, this collection of buildings was "our home."

TRADING IN OLD NELLIE

In the nineteenth century and well into the twentieth, farmers in Boulder County relied on draft animals to plant, cultivate and harvest their crops. Although it was oxen that pulled the covered wagons west in the mid-1860s, homesteaders were divided into two factions when it came to choosing between mules or horses to work their fields.

"Mules were used by a lot of people," said Roger King, "particularly for row crops." Mules were preferred for cultivating corn, tomatoes and cabbage because their small feet allowed them to walk the twenty inches between rows. Most of the Japanese farmers who operated truck farms in eastern Boulder County preferred mules. "A horse, with its larger hooves, would step on the plants and wipe out just about everything," King continued.

Although Evan Gould never owned mules, he recalled a day of haying near Niwot with a mule team belonging to Hugh and Alvah Dodd. When a sudden rainstorm came up, he was close enough to Walter Hogsett's lumberyard on Second Avenue to head for cover in their storage shed. "I backed [the team] up and was holdin' 'em," he laughed. "But they drug me right out there in that rain. I just had to stay and hang onto 'em," he continued. "If I turned 'em loose, I didn't know where they'd end up."

Many early photos of threshing crews in Boulder County depict draft horse teams harnessed to wagons piled high with grain bundles. In spite of the sepia tones of these old images, most of the horses appear to be gray or black. According to Roger King, they were Percherons, the predominant draft animal used here in the late 1800s. "This breed came from the Perche Valley of France," he explained. "They were later replaced by the Belgian horse, which was sorrel, bay or roan."

The importance of draft animals is apparent in this photograph of Jerome Gould. Horses, as well as family members, were often included in outdoor family portraits. *Courtesy of Niwot Historical Society.*

Evan Gould didn't mince words when describing the brief time he owned Belgians. "I thought they were prettier than the Percherons, but they were the orneriest and most worthless darn things that ever were," he laughed. His friend Budd Coniloque added, "They didn't have brain one in their heads."

When small tractors were introduced to local farmers, many argued that they were "too mechanical." Yet it was hard to deny the improvements when comparing them to a five-horse team hitched to a sixteen-bottom plow. "Three of those five-horse teams could plow about six acres in a day," Evan said. "But with a tractor, a farmer can cover ten acres in an hour." The day in 1944 when Evan traded five horses for his first tractor, dealer Walter Hogsett paid him $1,000. To seal the deal, however, Evan had to throw in his horse collars as well. He reluctantly agreed but refused to give up his harness. "I tell ya, I was sick," he muttered. "But I still had three horses left, and I worked 'em up until 1952 or 1953. Then I finally got rid of 'em."

To Market, To Market

An array of fresh colors and smells greets you as you approach the produce stand. There are baskets of brown eggs for a dollar, in addition to the usual fresh-picked fruits and vegetables. Mounds of shiny red strawberries are piled into wooden berry boxes, which had been tacked together earlier that morning by the farmer's children. Fifty cents a box seems reasonable, so you buy an extra one for snacking on the way home. Piled neatly on the counter are peas, cabbage and sweet corn. And if you ask, there might still be some freshly churned butter and fresh eggs as well.

No, you're not browsing among the crowded fruit stalls of today's farmers market in Boulder, Longmont or Niwot. You've stopped at a roadside stand somewhere in Boulder County in the 1920s or 1930s.

Young Rosalie (Rose) Allan's family farm stood along Valmont Road, just west of Seventy-fifth Street. A large portion of their income came from the sale of produce, dairy products, poultry and rabbits. Rose laughed as she recalled her role in the family enterprise. "We'd get up at daylight and pick peas," she said. "Dad would run water at night, and we'd get out in the morning and pick 'em barefoot because it was mud."

"I'll never forget the fate of one toad that got in my way," she laughed. "I stepped on him, and he got so far down in the mud [that] I don't think he ever knew what hit him."

Rose's father, Edwin Allan, traveled to Boulder each morning to deliver eggs, butter and produce to boardinghouses and private residences. One of his regular customers, Mrs. Temple, operated a student boardinghouse on Pine Street. (Folks familiar with 1980s television remember it today as the *Mork and Mindy* house.) Mrs. Temple often ordered fresh-dressed poultry or rabbits to serve to her boarders. Since Rose and her siblings raised and butchered the rabbits, they shared the profits among themselves. "We earned about $1.50 for a dressed rabbit," she recalled.

As the youngest boy in the family, Vernon Ewing was in charge of his family's watermelon business. "Every Sunday, Father loaded the wagon with melons and drove it down to the corner of Ninety-fifth Street and Arapahoe Road, where it remained until the last melon was sold," said Vernon. "The largest melons averaged about thirty-five pounds and sold for fifty cents apiece," he continued. After cutting open three or four melons to show their juicy red meat, Vernon settled down with a stack of his favorite magazines and waited for the customers to arrive.

"All those city folks would come out and buy watermelons every weekend," he explained. "It was a kind of hobby with the high school kids to steal watermelons from our field."

In those days, the produce selection may not have been as extensive as we find in our markets today, but it was farm fresh. And although no one promoted the fact, it was strictly organic.

GONE AND ALMOST FORGOTTEN

One of the largest buildings on Second Avenue was demolished almost fifty years ago. The two-story Livingston Hotel once stood on the site now occupied by the Niwot Emporium. During its heyday, it had many owners, housed a small beauty parlor and was home to families and single men who worked at various jobs nearby.

It wasn't until 1999 that the date of the hotel's construction was verified. Chellee Courtney, great-granddaughter of George Livingston, discovered old invoices and receipts confirming that it was 1907 when George hired Jim Hood to build Niwot's only hotel. Such a facility was needed to house railroad section crews and unmarried workers from the local alfalfa mill, creamery and flour mill. Overnight rooms were also available for visiting businessmen who were in town to inspect oil wells in the Boulder Oil Field west of Niwot.

Second Avenue must have been a beehive of activity in 1907, as John Nelson completed work on Nelson Hall (now the Left Hand Grange Hall) and began building the Niwot Mercantile building across the street.

All of George Livingston's business papers were dated 1907. They included bills for $119.00 to construct the front porch, $4.20 for foundation bricks and a Northwestern Fire and Marine Insurance Company policy insuring the building for $1,100.00.

No records have been found, however, to indicate who operated the hotel for the first few years. Livingston himself left town almost as soon as the hotel was completed. The widow of C.B. Allen briefly managed the facility after the death of her husband, and George Walden took it over in about 1916.

Luvesta Jones recalled that the place had bedbugs by the time Mattie and William Sutton became owners in 1921. Mattie provided meals in the dining room for boarders while William shoed horses in the lot next door. William was fatally kicked in the head by a customer's horse in 1922, but Mattie continued to run the hotel for several more years.

By the time the Livingston Hotel was razed, it had become an eyesore that townsfolk were glad to see removed. *Courtesy of Niwot Historical Society.*

Benjamin Shelley moved his family into the hotel in 1928. His wife, Goldie, established a beauty parlor on the first floor, where ladies came to have their hair *marcelled*. Meanwhile, Ben operated his barbershop in the pool hall next door. Hotel patrons were charged twenty-five cents to use the bathtub in back of his shop.

The Joseph Kroelick family was the last to occupy the building before it was demolished in the 1960s.

Part IV

SOCIAL CALENDAR

LETTING OFF STEAM

Weekends and holidays found folks tapping their toes and kicking up their heels at the many dance venues in Boulder, Longmont and various mountain communities. Young and old gathered at local granges, barns, schoolhouses or dance halls to socialize till the wee hours of the morning.

Niwot was home to several musical groups over the years. In addition to the Niwot Military Band, which performed in the town's bandstand in the early 1900s, there were the Jailbirds, the Melody Maids and Della Sullivan's orchestra from nearby Longmont.

"I played with Della for thirty years," Lee Forsythe recalled. "We'd even go from here over to North Park and play dances. That would be a whole day's trip in a little Model T." Della's band consisted of five musicians playing piano, drums, sax, trumpet and banjo. One can barely imagine stuffing five adults and their instruments into such a small vehicle. But by strapping Lee's drums onto the rear of the car, it could be done when necessary.

Doyle Jones recalled dances in the Hornbaker barn on Nimbus Road when he was a boy. "But those were during bootleg days," he laughed, "and drinking brawls often closed them down." Reverend Tillman continually chastised Frank Hornbaker for posting dance hall ads in the post office window.

By the time he was eighteen, Doyle and his future wife, Luvesta Ereckson, had organized their own group, the Jailbirds. "We even dressed in striped uniforms and hats," he chuckled. Luvesta accompanied them on piano while a very young Lee Forsythe sat in on drums. But according to Doyle, the best

Square dancing was also a part of the dance scene. The Left Hand Grange team competed with other county granges in the 1950s. *Photo from Left Hand Grange scrapbook.*

musician in his group was the versatile Cy Greenlee, who could play sax, violin and trumpet.

Of course, these young musicians didn't quit their day jobs. The hours were too long and the pay wasn't good. Dances often started about 9:00 p.m. and could last until 2:00 or 3:00 a.m., depending on the crowd. Folks in attendance sometimes took up a collection to entice the musicians to stay longer.

Lee remembered being paid $6.00 for an evening's work. But if the crowds didn't materialize, then payment was often in the form of leftover doughnuts and sandwiches. At first, the Melody Maids earned $2.50 apiece for the evening, but that amount increased tenfold after they became popular. Their fee was doubled for New Year's Eve performances. Musicians in Doyle and Luvesta's band made $5.00 a night plus $5.00 for their car. Although it doesn't sound like much, Doyle calculated, "We made $800.00 one year, and that was after we had worked all day on our milk route."

Niwot's First Rec Center

At the corner of Niwot Road and Seventy-third Street lies Dodd Lake, one of many local reservoirs created to store irrigation water. Hinman Ditch fills the lake each spring, and the water is released during the growing season to irrigate cropland across the road. Until 1999, the lake was owned by the Alvah Dodd family but is now Boulder County Parks and Open Space property.

Recreation centers are a modern phenomenon, and most rural communities did not have them. But for Niwot, there was always Dodd Lake. Children could fish for free, but adults had to belong to a club that leased the lake from the Dodd family. Their gear was stored in a small locked shed on the property.

In addition to muskrats, which were trapped by local youngsters, and little green turtles that were lovingly carried home as pets, Dodd Lake was stocked with sunfish, crappies and carp. No one ate carp, of course, but catching them could be fairly exciting. Don Spangler recalled grabbing them by hand during spawning season. "If you stood real still," he said, "they'd swim right up to you, and you could grab 'em by the tail." One three-footer dragged him about twenty feet across the lake before he finally let go.

In the winter, Dodd Lake was jumping on Friday and Saturday nights as boys and girls gathered along its north shore for ice-skating parties. Rubber tire bonfires provided warmth for the revelers, but Idell Leinweber cautioned that you had to stay downwind because it was pretty smelly. Wood fires were substituted when hot dogs, marshmallows and hot chocolate were on the menu.

Nancy Dodd Hindman's home was on the south shore of the lake. She still remembers lying in bed and listening to the loud thumping as the ice cracked and groaned. "We could see all the freeze cracks when we skated," she said.

In those days, the ice was often thick enough to support the weight of an automobile. Just imagine a line of skaters being pulled by an old car as it slid across the ice, swerving just enough to *crack the whip*. Such derring-do was likely concealed from parents, much as it would be today.

According to old-timers, at least one fisherman drowned in Dodd Lake. But perhaps the most memorable disaster occurred in the 1940s, when a herd of cattle broke through a fence and wandered onto the frozen lake in the middle of the night. As the animals grouped together, the ice gave way. Dr. William Harrison, a retired veterinarian from Longmont, still remembers that night. Dr. Bill, as he was known, had just established his practice when he and his partner got word of the emergency. "We worked all night long recovering those cattle," he explained.

"We put ropes on [the cattle] and slid them across the ice to shore," Dr. Bill continued. "The highway department came in with planking and built sleds so they could sled the animals as we brought them to shore." They were then bedded down in straw and given heated intravenous anti-ferments to prevent bloating.

"We were able to save the majority of the herd," he said. "I think we lost [only] five cattle that night."

Nothin' To Do

Some years ago, Gary Moschetti of Louisville wrote to Boulder's *Daily Camera*, commenting on complaints by teenagers that "there isn't anything to do" in Boulder. He then proceeded to list all the imaginative ways he and his friends amused themselves in the 1930s. If you've heard this same complaint from members of your own family, they might gain inspiration from other old-timers who grew up in Boulder County in the early 1900s. Despite having few organized entertainment venues in those days, youngsters always found ways to create their own fun.

Dances at grange halls all over the county seemed to be the universal choice for weekend entertainment. In addition to the Left Hand Grange in Niwot, the Boulder Valley and Altona Granges had Saturday night dances with live music. No booze was allowed, but it could usually be found outside in the parking lot. Chuck Waneka remembered going to dances with his family in the early 1930s. While the adults danced in one room, the children played in the other. When they ran out of steam, they curled up on piles of coats on the floor or on chairs lined up against the wall. There they'd sleep until it was time to go home.

Tagging along beside their parents when they settled their grocery tabs each month usually paid off with free candy. Reverend Taylor always had a candy jar on the counter of his White House grocery store, as did Bill Buchert across the tracks. Buchert's candy was suspect, however, and children soon learned to politely accept his jawbreakers and then stuff them in their pockets to be disposed of later. Most of them knew that a small hole in their candy meant that a critter lived inside. When Herb Atkins cracked his open, he found it full of worms that had devoured the center. He swore the candy was at least fifty years old.

Most youth activities in the Left Hand Valley revolved around ball teams, Sunday school, Junior Grange and 4-H. In the 1920s, these young girls were probably part of a local 4-H club. *Courtesy of Niwot Historical Society.*

Herb and Jack Slater were buddies growing up. Although they both had jobs after school, they found time to hike the countryside together and camped out as far away as the White Rocks, Haystack Mountain and Gunbarrel Hill.

Discovering litters of kittens hidden in the straw pile, grabbing the worm bucket from a nail on the back porch and hiking down to the fishing hole or shooting at magpies through a knot hole in the back of the barn—these were the ways children entertained themselves years ago.

Kids growing up in Niwot today are treated to most of the amenities any small town could offer. With Easter egg hunts, Halloween parades, ice cream socials, bike trails and ball fields, there's little reason to complain that "there's nothin' to do."

LUCKY FIND

As children, we often looked for four-leaf clovers when we played outside with friends. Such discoveries were considered good luck. And who among us hasn't bent down to pick up a stray coin on the sidewalk? It's not that such items bring us riches, but it's the sense of discovery that makes us look down occasionally in search of hidden treasures.

For Robin Grabowski, it was a glint of metal that caught her eye one summer as she tended her horses north of Lyons. When she bent down to brush away the dirt, she discovered what appeared to be a large silver-colored coin, measuring about two inches in diameter. Upon closer examination, she realized that she had just unearthed an object that had been lost for more than a century.

What she found that day was a medallion awarded by the Boulder County Agricultural Society for the best draft stallion exhibited at the 1872 county fair. The stamped logo on the face of the medal was still pristine, despite its age. One could clearly make out images of a walking plow and a miner's pick and shovel against a backdrop of the Rocky Mountains.

The Agricultural Society, a precursor to today's Boulder County Fair, was established in 1869 and was the first fair to be organized in Colorado Territory. It lasted only five years, however, before being replaced by the Industrial Association of Boulder. Each fall, the best crops, livestock and domestic science projects were exhibited in Boulder at the fairgrounds on Valmont Road between Twenty-eighth and Thirtieth Streets. Demonstrations of metal mining techniques were showcased as well, along with impressive mineral displays.

But who had won this medal back in 1872? Delicate hand engraving on the reverse side was still legible after more than a century in the abrasive sand and seasonal flooding of the nearby Little Thompson River. In more recent decades, it had also endured the continual trampling by livestock around the stock tank where it was found. The inscription read: "Awarded to D.J. Lykins, Best Draught Stallion, 1 yr old, 1872."

The recipient, David Johnson Lykins, is still referred to by local historians as Boulder County's first beekeeper. In 1849, at the age of twenty-one, he left his home in Indiana to join thousands of others in the historic California Gold Rush. There, he *struck it rich*. By the end of seven years, he had accumulated over $10,000, which was enough to return to the Midwest to take up a homestead near St. Joseph, Missouri.

Records show that Lykins came to Boulder County in 1859, one year after gold was discovered in the Gold Hill Mining District above Boulder. This time, however, he did not come to mine gold. Instead, he settled near the mouth of Left Hand Canyon to raise thoroughbred Shorthorn cattle. Today, this area still bears the names Lykins Canyon and Lykins Gulch.

Because he needed more land, Lykins purchased a large ranch along the Little Thompson River north of Lyons, where he built a home for his bride,

Ann Gilman. It was there that he lost the medallion that his young stallion had earned for him.

Today, this historic artifact survives not only as a symbol of the first fair in Colorado but also represents an early settler whose name remains part of Boulder County's agricultural history. Would this medallion have survived if David Lykins had not lost it more than 135 years ago?

KEEPER OF THE PAST

Niwot lost its unofficial town archivist when Doyle Hornbaker passed away in November 1989. He was ninety-one years old, but in his prime, he was the journalistic voice of the Left Hand Valley.

There was an unspoken responsibility placed on early newspaper editors, it seems. They were expected to be custodians of documents important to residents of the communities they served. Thus, *Niwot Tribune* editor Doyle Hornbaker became the quasi-official archivist of Niwot's historical photographs and artifacts. His detailed accounts continue to make it possible for researchers to date familiar buildings in town. His ads were an unofficial business directory for the period, and his social columns followed the travels, activities and accomplishments of local residents.

There were several local newspapers over the years. Although the *Niwot Weekly News* lasted only ten months in 1912, Niwot tidbits appeared in the Boulder and Longmont papers on a regular basis.

During the Depression, local bricklayer Pete Slater circulated a free alternative newspaper, the *Broadcaster*. His purpose was twofold: to provide merchants with an inexpensive medium for weekly ads and to provide a forum for his jokes and his Libertarian political views. He paid his young stepson, Herb Atkins, twenty-five cents to deliver the one-page sheet to town residents.

In August 1921, the first issue of the *Niwot Tribune* went to press. Its first editor, E.S. Hays, filled the first issue with business and social news, school information and a notice of the farewell sermon of Reverend Gale at the United Brethren Church. Advertisements included Bill Buchert's general store, Frank Monthey's garage, the Niwot State Bank, Livingston Hotel, Hogsetts' Lumber and Reverend Taylor's White House grocery store. In August 1946, Doyle Hornbaker became the *Tribune*'s new owner. As editor and linotype operator, he continued to keep the community informed of local news, coming events and available goods and services. He wrote of grange

Doyle Hornbaker was owner, editor and linotype operator for the *Niwot Tribune* from 1946 to 1958. *Courtesy of Niwot Historical Society.*

and Rebekah meetings, of residents' comings and goings, agricultural news and daily train schedules.

By Thursday, deadline day, Doyle had solicited ads from Niwot, Longmont and Boulder. Hometown news was reported on the front page, and the ads were arranged near the back. On Fridays, the *Tribune* hit the streets.

Doyle's nephew, Don Spangler, looked after his uncle in his declining years. When asked how Doyle gathered the local news, Don chuckled. "He walked around town and talked to people—snooped a lot. And people who had anything of interest would phone him or walk into the newspaper office and tell him," Don continued. "He'd find a place to put it in the paper."

The last issue of the *Tribune* was printed in 1958. Years later, Doyle donated his complete newspaper collection to Bobbie Lohmann and Idell Leinweber of the Niwot Historical Society. In 1987, they were loaned to the Colorado Historical Society for microfilming. Today, the fragile originals are in the archives of the Longmont Museum, the Niwot Historical Society and probably many private collections.

Pocket Change

The desire for a little spending money is universal among today's adolescents, and youngsters growing up in the nineteenth century were no exception.

Wildlife was abundant in Boulder County, and while their parents hunted bear, deer and elk to augment food supplies, young boys set traps for small animals and set their gun sights on waterfowl to send to market. From the earliest days, rabbits, coyotes, skunks and muskrats were plentiful along Boulder and St. Vrain Creeks.

Alonzo Allen and Walter Emery often hunted together on Lake Park in Longmont. The area attracted large flocks of ducks and wild geese—easy prey for two boys armed with muzzleloading shotguns. Sometimes they sold their game to buyers from Denver, but more often it was sent to the mining camps west of Boulder. The boys received fifteen cents for each cottontail

While some wildlife were hunted or trapped for food or pelts, predatory animals were often shot by farmers for protection of their livestock. Here, Niwot's Frank Burke has successfully eliminated at least one threat to his chickens. *Courtesy of Niwot Historical Society.*

rabbit, while jackrabbits were worth a quarter and large mallards brought fifty cents. Little by little, these coins added up to substantial spending money.

As a youth in the 1860s, Ernest Pease worked three or four traps near his home east of Boulder. He often caught muskrats on cold, wintry days by resetting the traps each morning and evening. Sometimes they were still alive when he walked his trap line, but usually they were frozen stiff.

In the early 1900s, Evan Gould trapped muskrats in the lakes and irrigation ditches around Niwot. He carefully skinned them and paid an extra fifteen cents for insurance before shipping the pelts to a fur company in Denver. As he explained, the proper skinning technique was essential: "You had to be awful careful not to make a hole in 'em, because they were just about ruined then."

There was no guarantee that only muskrats would be lured into his traps, however. "We got a skunk one morning," Evan chuckled, "and we went on to school thinking we had the skunk all [washed] off us, but we didn't. So they set us clear off in a corner where we wouldn't bother anybody."

When the United States entered World War II, the army began purchasing muskrat pelts to line aviator helmets. As the market price of muskrats skyrocketed to almost five dollars, more and more trappers gathered along the creek banks. This time, they weren't just youngsters.

Today, muskrats, geese and ducks abound on local lakes and streams. But due to the loss of suitable wildlife habitat on the plains of Boulder County, other species of game birds have declined. Permits are now required for trapping, and young boys have found other ways to earn a little spending money.

FASHIONABLE FLOUR SACKS

In the early part of the twentieth century, bloomers were standard issue for girls' basketball teams. The fashion concept had been around since 1851, when Amelia Bloomer began promoting the costume that still bears her name. At that early date, bloomers composed the bottom half of an outfit that consisted of a knee-length dress over a pair of caftan-style pants.

Despite the fact that they allowed more freedom of movement, the style provoked much ridicule and criticism. Their popularity didn't revive until the widespread use of bicycles in the late 1880s, when a more liberating form of apparel was demanded.

Mary Hummel Wells recalled the first time she ever saw fancy sateen bloomers. "My dad was secretary of the North Boulder Farmers Ditch," she explained, "and Mrs. Williamson had come [to the front door] to pay her dues." According to Mary, Mrs. Williamson always wore a flowing black skirt and floppy black hat. But the most memorable occasion was when she arrived on the front porch while fending off a gust of wind.

"One hand was on the floppy hat and the other was trying to hold down her skirt," Mary laughed. "But the thing that impressed me was that she had the most beautiful green sateen bloomers underneath that skirt."

For many rural families in the 1920s, times were hard, and girls like Mary wore simple bloomers fashioned from flour sacks. "Sometimes you could still read the flour label on the pants," Mary recalled.

Longmont's Golden West Flour Company was aware of the recycling of their feed sacks by housewives, so they included a bleaching formula in the recipe pamphlet distributed to their customers. In part, it read:

> *Do not use kerosene or oil to remove printing from cotton flour sacks.*
> *Wash in soap and hot water, rubbing the printed surface on a scrubbing board.*
> *Rinse and then boil the sack in strong suds for half an hour.*
> *Then rinse and wring out.*

Members of the 1916 Niwot girls' basketball team wore traditional uniforms with white middies, bloomers and long black stockings. The hair bow was optional. *Courtesy of Niwot Historical Society.*

For the removal of any residual ink, they advised dipping the sack in Javelle water, a concoction made by passing chlorine gas through a solution of sodium carbonate. It seems that pioneer homemakers benefitted from a basic knowledge of chemistry.

NIWOT'S OLD-TIME FIDDLER

Before he passed away in 1992 at the age of ninety-four, Clarence Conilogue was one of Niwot's best-known musicians. He was part of a long musical tradition. Many before him had played in the Niwot Military Band or were affiliated with one of several local dance bands in the 1920s and 1930s. But Clarence often performed solo.

Clarence and his brothers, known to friends as Con, Toots, Budd and Babe, spent their childhood on a farm east of Niwot. Like most rural youngsters growing up in the early 1900s, their days were filled with farm

Although slowed a bit by a stroke, Clarence still held his own at a Niwot Nostalgia Days celebration in 1990, when he shared the stage with banjo artist Pete Wernick of Niwot. *Courtesy of Niwot Historical Society.*

chores at home and classes at the Beasley School near their farm. But there was time for fun as well. The boys loved baseball and played for many years on the Niwot Farmers baseball team.

Their father, Edward, was a road overseer for the Beasley road district. In the evenings, he played his fiddle for the family's entertainment. By the time Clarence was eight years old, he was playing too. Encouraged by his parents, Clarence took weekly fiddle lessons from a teacher he called "Old Man Hatch" in Longmont—an advantage his father probably never had.

Fiddle music was Clarence's passion but not his livelihood. At the age of eighteen, just days before his high school graduation, he took the postal exam and was hired to deliver the mail along Rural Route #1 west of Niwot. His association with the postal service lasted for forty-two years, and during that time, he missed only six days because of bad weather.

Clarence lost his first wife, Susan, in 1933. Rachel, his second wife, was a musician and accompanied him on the piano for the rest of his fiddling days. Whether it was for a square dance at the grange or an impromptu living room performance with friends, her chording kept Con in step and in tune.

When asked to play a tune, Clarence invariably chose his favorites, "The Wabash Cannonball" and "Pretty Redwing," sometimes reciting the lyrics as he played.

After listening to a recording of Clarence at age ninety, Niwot banjo artist Pete Wernick observed, "He's got real tone. If he's a shell of his former self, then his former self was pretty darn good."

JAKE

Few folks living in Niwot today remember Jake, but he was once a very vocal member of the community. Although he was only three years old in the late 1930s, Jake's vocabulary was already colorful enough to catch even the most seasoned listener off guard.

He lived in the basement of the house now occupied by Niwot Dental at the corner of Second Avenue and Niwot Road. Lest you wonder why the Spartan living conditions, I should explain that Jake was Herb Atkins's pet magpie. Herb found him in 1937, alone in a nest in an old cottonwood tree along Dry Creek. When he brought him home to the house he shared with his mother, Evelyn Slater, she determined that the bird should be consigned to the basement.

Jake grew quickly on a diet of fried eggs and bread with a little bit of gravel mixed in. He spent his days roosting in the basement or, because the windows were kept open, flying around the neighborhood at will. Herb never worried about Jake's whereabouts because he would inevitably be chased home by the flocks of crows that frequented Niwot in those days.

As with any young animal, Herb talked to his new pet, never anticipating the day when Jake would talk back to him. The conversations (or perhaps soliloquies would be a better term) began with the usual "Good morning," "Hello" and "How are you?" Bessie Atkinson, who lived next door, didn't appreciate the loud calls emanating from Herb's house each morning. "Run, Bessie, run," Jake would scream at the top of his lungs. And Don Spangler, who delivered the *Denver Post* in Niwot at that time, still remembers Jake yelling and laughing at him as he passed by on his bicycle.

From his roost in the basement, Jake observed the world outside. "He whistled at dogs passing by and drove 'em nuts," Don recalled. "And when he called 'kitty, kitty, kitty,' every cat in town would come over and look at him, then walk away in frustration."

"I couldn't teach him to cuss in front of Ma," Herb explained, "so I had to whisper the words to him." He chuckled as he recalled how Jake learned to swear, but never above a whisper.

Jake began to pester Herb's mother one day when she went down to the basement. She scolded him as she pushed him away and then went back upstairs. Soon, the sound of breaking glass sent her rushing back

Evelyn Slater and her son, Herb Atkins, lived at the intersection of Second Avenue and Niwot Road. *Courtesy of Niwot Historical Society.*

downstairs, where she found Jake systematically pushing empty canning jars off the shelves. As she confronted him once again, Jake began laughing and whispered, "Go to hell. Go to hell."

That colorful phrase probably saved Jake's life on the day he flew into Frank Reeves's cherry orchard. Frank was standing among the trees with his shotgun aimed at crows, which were rapidly consuming his crop. As Herb rode up on his bicycle, he asked, "You didn't shoot my magpie did you?" Reeves replied, "No, I didn't shoot him. He told me to go to hell."

In September 1940, Herb Atkins joined the army and left Jake behind in the care of his mother. Perhaps missing his longtime buddy, Jake slipped away and never returned. Or perhaps his mother had simply closed the basement window.

Niwot's Music Makers

Music played a big part in early communities throughout Boulder County. Even the smallest towns had a brass or military band. These were not professional musicians but local music makers who came together for public gatherings and festive occasions.

Some were fortunate to have been influenced by schoolteachers who were willing and able to teach them. Marie Tyrer, who taught in several mountain schools, and Dorris Steele, who influenced her Superior students, offered private lessons or encouraged pupils to participate in band or orchestra rehearsals before and after school. Their communities supported their efforts by donating or lending instruments to the aspiring young musicians and attending their concerts and recitals. Some students continued their musical studies in high school and went on to participate in community or professional bands after graduation.

Other musicians were in great demand for Saturday night dances in barns and grange halls throughout the county. These events often lasted into the wee hours of the morning with only periodic breaks for doughnuts and punch. Of course, there were always those who preferred to adjourn to the parking lot to drink beer and compete for the attention of the girls. Many old-timers recount their courtship days, which began at the jitney dances in Longmont or at square dances in the Left Hand Grange Hall.

Although most communities held concerts in the town park, Niwot's bandstand jutted out into Second Avenue, just east of the railroad crossing. Its platform was elevated a few feet off the ground and was

This was the first official group photograph of the Niwot military band, taken in 1912. Its leader at the time was farmer John Hill, seated at the far right in the second row. Military bands were limited to only brass and percussion instruments. *Courtesy of Niwot Historical Society.*

reached by a narrow set of stairs. A flagpole extended several feet above the peak of its roof.

In 1912, Niwot heard its military band for the first time. The *Niwot Weekly News* described it as "one of the best little bands in the county, and though organized only a few months [ago], it is already a credit to the town that supports it."

That first group of musicians, with few exceptions, was composed of young men from farming families in the Left Hand Valley. Of its nineteen members, six were Johnsons and three were Dodds. The group rehearsed in the grange hall, which at that time was a small wooden building at the west end of town.

Following his years with the Niwot band, Royce Johnson continued to entertain locally. After retiring from farming, he and his wife played ragtime music on dual pianos at the Stanley Hotel in Estes Park. "To look at his huge hands," Evan Gould recalled, "you wonder how he could even *play* a piano."

The Niwot Military Band dissolved in the 1930s, and its bandstand stood in disrepair until the local garden club resurrected it. After cutting off its rotted legs, they moved it from the center of Second Avenue, surrounded it with flower beds and transformed it into a picnic shelter.

Part V

EARLY ORGANIZATIONS

A FAITHFUL CONGREGATION

When settlement of the Left Hand Valley began in the 1860s, homesteaders were somewhat isolated from one another as they proved up their land. Their need for social contact resulted in the formation of several religious, fraternal and educational groups, which met in private homes or one-room schoolhouses.

Five years before the town of Niwot was platted, followers of the United Brethren faith established what the Colorado Business Directory called the "Left Hand United Brethren Church." Although they had no sanctuary, the congregation gathered for services in the tiny schoolhouse on the Dan Burch property whenever a traveling minister came through the area. They continued meeting there until the school board deemed it inappropriate to hold religious services in a public building. Their dilemma was solved, however, when parishioner Henry Hornbaker purchased the building and leased it back to the Brethren.

Weary of relying on others' generosity, the rapidly expanding congregation began a pledge drive to construct a church. Ninety-six parishioners stepped forward to cover building expenses, and the Alvah Dodd family donated a portion of their land northwest of Niwot. Two hundred members and friends gathered for its dedication on April 3, 1892. No longer dependent on occasional visits by circuit riders, they could now hire their own pastor and house him in an adjoining parsonage.

The church building was moved in 1912, to the corner of Franklin and Third Avenue in Niwot. When Amy Sherman tried to imagine her father,

The United Brethren Church with its classic New England–style architecture stood in stark contrast to the simpler farmsteads around it. The tiny parsonage next door was reminiscent of many vernacular homes still standing in old town Niwot. *Courtesy of Niwot Historical Society.*

Charles Sherman, and Bud Tucker moving the heavy frame building to town with a team of horses, she concluded that "they must have skidded it."

Tragedy struck when the church caught fire in 1951. Thwarted by an inner space created after a brick veneer was added to the original frame siding, firemen were unable to direct water to the flames inside. Although the building was a total loss, parishioners managed to salvage the organ, a piano and the chancel pews, all of which sustained damage.

Within a year, its 172 members rebuilt their church, although another change was waiting around the corner. The parent United Brethren Church, which had already merged with the Evangelical Church in 1946, merged again in 1968 with the Methodist Church. By 1970, the Niwot congregation had sold its church building and moved to 7405 Lookout Road, where it remains today.

On October 3, 2010, the Niwot United Methodist Church commemorated the 140 years since the first United Brethren congregation first met in the tiny schoolhouse on the Dan Burch farm.

A Gardener's Scrapbook

Another Niwot tradition quietly slipped away in November 1998, when, after sixty years, the Niwot Home and Garden Club disbanded. During those years, this remarkable group of ladies designed and maintained a beautiful community garden at the corner of Second Avenue and Murray Street.

From the time the club was organized in 1938, membership was limited to twenty-five so that meetings could be held in members' homes. Anyone absent for three consecutive meetings was dropped from the roll to make room for others on a long waiting list.

"We Sow, We Grow, We Show" was the theme for their 1953 flower show at the Left Hand Grange Hall. Ribbons were awarded by visiting judges for botanical categories similar to those at the county fair. Monthly programs ranged from studying new floral varieties and flower arranging to creating tray decorations for patients at Fitzsimons Army Hospital in Denver. For years, the Niwot club belonged to the Colorado Federation of Garden Clubs and participated in their statewide, as well as local, activities.

Their most enduring project came in 1946, with the creation of a community garden. By that time, Niwot had two hundred residents, and

Some members preferred house dresses to overalls while preparing the community garden for planting. *Photo from Niwot Garden Club scrapbook.*

passenger traffic at the depot was brisk. Travelers arriving by train were greeted by an ugly vacant lot across the tracks that had become a dumping ground for trash. Weeds had gained the upper hand, and the sun-baked soil was laced with cinders from years of passing steam locomotives.

Determined to beautify the entrance to their community, the ladies of the garden club launched a project that took them years to complete. The site presented a daunting challenge. The Colorado & Southern Railroad did not permit planting within twenty feet of the track, and the telegraph company allowed no trees to be placed under their lines.

Working within those restrictions, a site plan was drawn up with paths outlined with river rock radiating outward from the center toward Murray Street and Second Avenue. A rose garden and annual and perennial flower beds were penciled in. Flowering trees and evergreens rounded out the sketch plan. Expenses would be funded by plant sales, bake sales and donations.

Little was accomplished the first year except to remove loads of trash, burn off the tumbleweeds and plow and level the ground.

The following spring, a well was dug. Only a posthole digger was needed to reach the high water table underlying the entire town. After a hydrant was installed, planting began. The derelict bandstand on the corner was dragged to the middle of the garden, where it was transformed into a beautiful picnic shelter.

The entire community enjoyed the garden for many years. But by the time the railroad sold the land for commercial development in the 1970s, its original *bloom* had disappeared. Aging club members could no longer keep up with watering and cultivation chores. Yet throughout its lifetime, the Niwot Community Garden was a source of community pride.

125 Years of Community Support

Folks in Niwot take the Left Hand Grange Hall for granted. Whenever space is needed for a meeting, potluck, concert or dance, the grangers generously accommodate almost all reasonable requests.

The grange hall's presence in Niwot is so significant that, according to the architectural guidelines drawn up for the Niwot Historic District in 1993, no new building can be built higher than its thirty-foot roofline.

But do we really understand what a unique organization it is? Perhaps taking a look at its origin here in the Left Hand Valley will provide a new perspective and appreciation of its importance to Niwot and to Colorado as well. At the time Left Hand Grange #9 was organized in 1873, it was only the third in Boulder County and (as its title suggests) the ninth to be established in all of Colorado Territory.

The emergence of the grange movement (known nationally as the Patrons of Husbandry) coincided with a difficult period for American farmers. Bank failures and economic depression followed the Panic of 1873. In addition, Colorado Territory was under siege from a devastating grasshopper plague.

The organizational meeting of Left Hand Grange was held in the one-room Batchelder School at Sixty-third and Monarch Road. Its nineteen charter members included Porter Hinman, who, in just another two years, would plat the town of Niwot. After outgrowing the schoolhouse, the grange purchased Bethany Chapel west of town for its meeting hall.

Needing still more space, the grange raised money to build its own hall at the west end of Second Avenue by selling shares in the newly established Niwot Building and Investment Company. All went well until about 1920, when one granger announced that he had purchased nearly all the capital stock of deceased members. As a majority stockholder, he then declared that he intended to take possession of the building and convert it to a residence. Not surprisingly, the remaining grangers resisted. With a generous loan from member Frank Bolton, they purchased the outstanding stock and saved the hall from closure. The offending granger was summarily dropped from the membership.

The hall eventually became unusable and was moved to the Alvah Dodd farm for a granary. Attendance dwindled to just thirty members, who met only occasionally in homes or churches. By 1945, however, membership had increased, and meetings were moved to the large upstairs room in Nelson Hall. Satisfied with the comfort and convenience of the new location, Left Hand Grange purchased the hall in September of that year.

Today, Left Hand Grange #9 is the oldest active grange in Colorado. What is the reason for its longevity? In these times of declining agriculture in Boulder County, its members have adapted their outreach mission to accommodate contemporary needs. They have not lost sight of their responsibility to the community they serve.

LEFT HAND MEN'S CLUB

In 1960, Niwot was functioning much as it had for decades, except that the town newspaper had ceased publication and the train no longer stopped for passengers and freight. Real estate activity was slow, however, and the few

Members of the Left Hand Grange #9, pictured here in 1888, included farmers from distant areas of the county who would later organize their own granges. The sashes and aprons signify grange officers. *Courtesy of Niwot Historical Society.*

businesses remaining in town were barely getting by. Niwot was still very much an agricultural town, even though Boulder County had officially lost its ranking as an agricultural county. Was Niwot ready for the changes that were coming?

Details of a proposed new Diagonal Highway between Boulder and Longmont were circulating among the locals, and work had already begun on Niwot's new water district. In addition, rumor had it that IBM was finally going to build on the 604 acres it had purchased northeast of Boulder.

When IBM did arrive in 1965, the effects were felt throughout the Left Hand Valley. New families were arriving almost weekly, and business activity in Niwot was on the rise.

As the population grew, an informal group of local businessmen and farmers began monthly dinner meetings at Nita's Café on Second Avenue. They called themselves the Left Hand Men's Club, and Bill Anderson from IBM was its first president. What began as a social club, however, soon took on a more important role. According to Dick Hicks and Mike Holubec, "We decided that it was a pretty good little group, and maybe we could do some things for the community."

One of their first projects was to organize a Little League baseball program. "There were kids that needed to play baseball," Holubec recalled. Community volunteers coached and organized games with neighboring

The Left Hand Men's Club street improvement project along Second Avenue was in full swing in 1961. Preliminary work included excavation for a gas line running the length of the street. *Courtesy of Niwot Historical Society.*

towns for a year or two. But they realized the need for more expertise and joined forces with a University of Colorado work-study program.

Their second project came about because Second Avenue was still dirt and gravel when the club organized. Members successfully approached county officials about sharing the cost of street paving. The only objection came from Francis Curtis, who operated an auto repair shop and confectionary shop next to the *Tribune* building. Curtis was outnumbered, however, and paving continued until the project was completed—well, almost. "Half of the street in front of his place was still gravel," Hicks chuckled. "And that's the way it was for quite a while."

Perhaps the most important men's club project occurred in 1968, when a special meeting was called to organize a volunteer fire department. Of the twenty-five men present, almost everyone signed up to volunteer. Most had little experience, if any, except for Mike Holubec and Pete Plantiga, who were volunteer firemen before moving with IBM to Colorado.

The Left Hand Men's Club gradually faded from existence, as did the Niwot Commercial Club back in 1912. But like the current Niwot Business Association, which was organized in 1992, each has contributed to the growth and stability of the greater Niwot community.

OLD ENGINE #10

It's a service we take for granted today—our local fire department. But until the late 1960s, Niwot's fire protection came from Longmont, which at the time had only one truck assigned to rural calls.

All of that changed in 1968, when the Left Hand Men's Club formed Niwot's volunteer fire department. Only Mike Holubec and Pete Plantiga had any previous experience, however, so they were chosen to conduct a training program. "We had training sessions at the Left Hand Water office," Holubec recalled, "where we taught some of the fundamentals of firefighting." When the two men reached the limit of their expertise, they collaborated with the St. Vrain School District's Outdoor Education program to bring instructors in from the Denver Fire Department.

The first order of business was construction of a firehouse. A financial campaign was launched, and a ninety-nine-year lease was signed with Left Hand Grange to build the facility on their property. It was dedicated during the first Niwot Nostalgia Days celebration in 1969.

The department's first fire truck was Engine #10, which was reassigned from Longmont Fire District. The old Chevy was one of four fire engines purchased by the county in 1946 and was originally assigned to Mead and then to Longmont, where it was used to cover rural fires.

Because Red Southern worked second shift at the new IBM plant, he became the department's first day captain. "We may have had fifteen to twenty volunteers, but during the day they were all working," Red explained. "Sometimes you were the only one on the truck because nobody else would show up."

Women from the fire department auxiliary were often pressed into service for daytime calls. "When I was day captain of the crew," Dick Hicks recalled, "we were having problems with train fires. We suspected the train crew was settin' them just to see the fire department run, because my crew was six women." But the ladies took their revenge on the day the train stopped and backed up to the Niwot crossing. According to Hicks, the engineer leaned out of the cab and made a smart remark to the volunteer working the fire hose. "The gal on the nozzle just lifted it up," he laughed, "and shot him right out of his seat."

Their most memorable fire occurred on January 7, 1969, when they were called to assist Boulder with a stubborn grass fire near Seventy-fifth and Arapaho Road. High winds had forced an airplane down at that location, and two fires were ignited. Southern remembered the event clearly. "There

Engine #10 was decked out every Fourth of July for the parade down Second Avenue. Dick Hicks and Mike Holubec always looked forward to getting behind the wheel once again for the annual event. *Courtesy of the author.*

for a while the winds were holdin' steady at 160 miles an hour with gusts to 180," he recalled.

When the new Mountain View Fire Station was built east of Niwot in 1982, Engine #10 stayed behind in the old firehouse. It had been four years since its last fire call.

"It's capable of fighting fires if need be," Southern explained, "even though it holds a very limited supply of water."

Niwot Sports

Although it was sixty years before the passage of Title IX, which legislated equality of public school sports programs for both sexes, Niwot already had a girls' basketball team in the 1910s. Eligibility was reserved for high school girls only, but at that time, Niwot elementary school included high school freshman and sophomore classes on the second floor.

No records exist to describe player qualifications, if indeed there were any. But for those girls who made the team, it must have been a thrill to dress for games in their fashionable shirtwaists, neckties and bloomers.

The strained budgets of most small school districts in Boulder County didn't cover the cost of team uniforms, although Niwot may have been a bit wealthier than some. School budgets were determined by county tax receipts, and the Colorado & Southern Railroad contributed substantially to School District #7 coffers. In all likelihood, however, Mom and Dad shelled out the money and considered it a school expense.

Since there was no indoor gymnasium, games and practice sessions were played outside on the playground. Whether an organized intramural program existed is unknown, but games were arranged between neighboring school districts from time to time.

There was no comparable school basketball team for the boys, but many of Niwot's young men were actively involved in the town's baseball team, the Niwot Farmers. Home games were played in an open field between Murray and Franklin Streets and First Avenue and Niwot Road. Like many small-town teams, its players wore official game uniforms. Pitcher Doyle Jones

The Niwot Farmers pose on the ball field bleachers. In the distance is the Niwot alfalfa mill along Niwot Road. *Courtesy of Niwot Historical Society.*

lamented that, unlike games played in Boulder, "There was no place to hang out after the games. Everyone came in cars and just went home."

In 1914, some local fans contacted the manager of the fledgling Northern Colorado Baseball League with hopes of entering the Farmers in the organization. With Charlie Taylor pitching and Forest Johnson catching, the boys were considered primed for the *big leagues*. No mention of the story was ever printed in the newspaper, however, so the ending to that story is lost to history.

Part VI

ENTERING THE
TWENTIETH CENTURY

COLORADO SUGAR

Before 1900, farmers in Boulder County relied primarily on the sale of poultry and dairy products to provide cash for seed, equipment and family necessities. But in 1903, something happened to change all that. Sugar beets were introduced to Colorado.

The success of the state's first sugar beet factory in Grand Junction, built in 1899, encouraged Great Western Sugar Company to build a second plant in Loveland just two years later. In 1903, the Longmont factory was built.

Flora Ewing, whose family farmed east of Boulder, wrote in her memoirs about company agents who came through the country to sign farmers for beet acreage. Her father was among many who contracted to plant three acres that first year. After a successful harvest and the security of a guaranteed market, he increased his acreage the following year.

Sugar beets proved more difficult to raise than hay or grain crops, however, and demanded attention throughout the growing season. Each acre required approximately one hundred hours of labor, three-fourths of it by hand. At first, family members performed the necessary planting, thinning, weeding, digging and topping of the beets. But as larger fields were planted, they could no longer keep up.

Before migrant labor was introduced, fieldworkers were difficult to find. Great Western knew that in order to maintain a high volume of beets for processing, the labor problem would have to be solved. They suggested hiring high school boys during the summer, but Flora described how their "scuffling and quarreling" in her father's fields often destroyed large patches of tender young plants. The most reliable workforce proved to be men from nearby coal mining towns who were idled when the mines closed down for the summer.

By October, the beets were ready to be harvested. Yet fall weather could be fickle, and in 1929, the beet crop froze in the ground before it could be dug. A drought in 1954 prevented the beets from maturing. Heavy rains caused problems as well, often forcing farmers to abandon their tractors for draft horses, which performed better in muddy fields.

Once beets were out of the ground, excess dirt dislodged and leafy tops removed, they were loaded into wagons and hauled to the nearest beet dump. Dumps were located at almost every railroad crossing. If an empty Great Western boxcar wasn't waiting on a siding to be filled, the beets were dumped onto the ground until a beet car arrived. They were then pitched by hand into the cars using four-pronged beet forks.

The Niwot dump was an elevated ramp where wagons could be emptied directly into a boxcar below. Evan Gould described the first time he drove his team over the top. "The horses were pretty spooky," he explained. "They got used to it, but every time I was up on top there, it seemed like a train had to come along."

The sides of Walter Kneale's sugar beet wagon were hinged, allowing him to dump his load onto the growing beet pile along the tracks north of Niwot. *Courtesy of Niwot Historical Society.*

Entering the Twentieth Century

Both world wars caused severe labor shortages as farm boys enlisted in the armed services. In order to sustain the industry, Great Western built a dormitory in Longmont to house a unique source of beet labor. About two hundred Italian prisoners of war were transported from a POW camp in Scottsbluff, Nebraska, to help with the 1943 harvest. German prisoners from Camp Carson replaced them the following year.

The Longmont plant closed permanently in 1977. Its dependable labor source was gone, and sufficient irrigation water was a thing of the past. However, its buildings remain on Sugar Mill Road southeast of Longmont, and the Great Western dormitory still stands at Third Avenue and Kimbark.

Telling Stories Out of School

Schoolchildren today share many of the same experiences that their ancestors faced more than a century ago. Yet the idea of walking two miles to school every day, sometimes in severe weather and with the added *thrill* of encountering wildlife along the way, is probably beyond their comprehension.

Marie Stengel was sometimes late for class at the Valmont School if Mr. Hunter's bull planted himself on the other side of the bridge she had to cross each morning. Her only option was to wait for him to wander to another part of the pasture.

Irene Smith was occasionally delayed by rattlesnakes on her way to the Potato Hill School west of Haystack Mountain. She and her friends carried garden hoes to dispatch the rattlers that wouldn't move out of their way.

Being slight of build, Mabel Andre relied on Charles Kelsey to hold her hand as they walked to school on windy days. If he didn't, she risked being blown into the ditch alongside the road.

Mabel always considered herself a troublemaker. She still recalls the day she was to report after school for whispering in class. But that afternoon, a spark from the chimney ignited the roof of the one-room Davidson schoolhouse, and it quickly burned to the ground. Although her punishment was instantly forgotten by the teacher, Mabel remembers her anxiety to this day.

When the wind howled down Left Hand Canyon, Frank Gould and his brother helped their young teacher, Mrs. Campbell, reach the Altona School. Without their assistance, she couldn't remain upright long enough to get there on her own. Many times, they were turned back, and school was canceled for the day.

Ina Jenner told of a classmate at the Pleasant View School who dreaded the punishment he was to receive the following day. Knowing that Mrs. Zingg intended to paddle him, he came to class armed with a pie pan tucked inside the seat of his trousers. The resulting clang when her hand hit his backside enraged her so much that she slapped his face in frustration.

Clarence Conilogue described being sent with his older brothers to the Beasley School in 1901. At four years of age, he was not yet eligible to enroll, but as he told it, it was only when he began reciting multiplication tables in his sleep that his parents withdrew him until the following year.

Allen Bolton lived with his family along Niwot Road, just west of Dodd Lake. He attended Batchelder School, southwest of Niwot, and vividly recalled the day he sat gazing out of the classroom window at smoke rising in the distance. When he realized that wind was blowing a grass fire toward his family's barn and haystack, he was out of the door in seconds. Their neighbor, Hattie Walton, had tossed stove ashes out her back door that day, not realizing they were still hot. As a result of a moment's carelessness, the Bolton barn lay in ruins, and their winter supply of cattle feed was destroyed.

Allen later attended the Niwot School and told of the day that he and Willard Blanton ran to Reverend Taylor's grocery store for candy during their lunch hour. It was almost one o'clock before they realized they had stayed too long to return to class before Miss Pierson rang the bell. To their good fortune, a train was slowly passing through town at the time, and as it gathered steam, the boys scrambled aboard. The schoolhouse was upon them in no time, and without hesitation, they jumped from the train as it sped past the schoolyard. Scraped, bruised and out of breath, they burst into the classroom, where Miss Pierson was waiting, strap in hand. Only the delightful flavor of Reverend Taylor's candy saved their field trip from being a total disaster.

Turn of Another Century

As Niwot enters the twenty-first century, the future looks promising. When it approached the twentieth century, the future must have looked favorable as well. The pace was definitely slower in 1900, but merchants were busy, and activity around the depot was fairly steady. Seven trains stopped each day for mail, farm products and passengers.

The commercial district was undergoing radical changes in 1905, as merchants began moving to the east side of the tracks. This initiated a building boom along Second Avenue and, for a time, businesses existed on both sides of the railroad tracks.

Swedish-born John Nelson had been a wagon maker in Niwot prior to 1900. When the business migration began, however, he turned his skills to carpentry and constructed two of the first commercial buildings along Second Avenue. The first was Nelson Hall on the corner of Franklin Street. There, he maintained an apartment for himself and rented out the rest of the building. The second was a mercantile almost directly across the street. Amy Sherman recalled that Nelson always had a cigar in his mouth and a gold pocket watch dangling from a chain.

There were several lodges in town at the time: the Odd Fellows, Rebekahs, Modern Woodmen and Royal Neighbors all met upstairs in Nelson Hall. Left Hand Grange was meeting in Batchelder School west of town, but members were raising money for a hall of their own. To do so, they sold stock through the Niwot Building and Investment Company, a corporation they had established in 1891. The money they raised was sufficient to fund construction of a small frame building west of the flour mill on Second Avenue.

Frank Bader was postmaster prior to 1900. His Victorian-style home is still standing on the corner of Franklin Street and Second Avenue. Today,

Nelson Hall was the tallest building in Niwot in 1910, and it remains so today. Niwot Historic District regulations, enacted in 1993, dictate that no new construction can be taller than its height of thirty feet. *Courtesy of Niwot Historical Society.*

it is part of an upscale restaurant complex surrounded by huge cottonwood trees and a dining patio. Nels Lind was section foreman for the railroad at the time and lived with his family in the section house south of the depot. Eric Ereckson was constable, and Henry Burch represented his Left Hand Valley constituents on the board of county commissioners. Burch also served on the local school board, which supervised the building of Niwot's new Willowdale School on Niwot Road and Franklin Street.

When the *Niwot Weekly News* was introduced in 1912, its first editorial painted a glowing picture of the town's economic health. "Niwot the beautiful—the center of a rich farming district where financial depressions are unheard of: where gilt-edged investments abound; where the old enjoy rest and quietude; where health and prosperity dwelleth; where public spirit animates." Its editor, Glenn Conkling, even erroneously predicted that Niwot's incorporation was imminent.

History for Sale

The old Ryssby schoolhouse at 9397 North Sixty-third Street is for sale. Within its walls lie the memories of children who attended classes there for over fifty years. Will the next owner be curious about its historic past?

Built in 1910, it was actually the third school built in Ryssby District #26. The first was made of logs and dated from 1872. The second was a one-room brick building constructed in 1888. The third schoolhouse, the one for sale today, dates from 1910. Also built of brick, it was later coated with stucco. Over time, as the student population increased, it was enlarged three times—first with an entryway, then a second floor and finally a basement.

The entryway accommodated coats, boots, lunchboxes and a water bucket, which was filled each morning from a cistern in the schoolyard. A communal dipper allowed students to fill their personal drinking cups, which were taken home at the end of each week to be washed. Andrew Steele recalled that most of his classmates were Swedish and spoke only "Swede" on the playground. Lessons were taught in English, but it frustrated the teachers who couldn't communicate in the Swedish language.

In about 1920, a second-story teacherage was added. Bertha James was the first teacher to occupy the new living quarters. There was no plumbing, however, so household water had to be hauled upstairs and waste water carried down in a slop jar.

Entering the Twentieth Century

The gradual consolidation of many small county school districts began in 1948, when the Bader, Altona, Ryssby and Potato Hill districts were combined into one. Students transferred to the larger Ryssby School while all the others were closed. To accommodate the combined enrollment, a basement was dug, and a lunchroom program was introduced. Final consolidation of all school districts in Boulder County was completed in the 1960s, resulting in the creation of the current St. Vrain Valley and Boulder Valley school districts.

Ryssby was never actually a town, but it *was* the first Swedish settlement in Colorado, dating from 1869. Aside from its stone church and stucco schoolhouse, no historic buildings remain. The former parsonage directly across the road from the Ryssby Lutheran Church was sold only a few years ago. Folks came from miles around to attend the huge farmyard auction, where hundreds of farm and household items were sold to the highest bidders. But before anyone could document the historic value of the farmhouse, an act that might have prevented its destruction, it was demolished. All that remain on the property today are its mailbox, a shed, a decaying silo and towering shade trees planted by parishioners over a century ago.

The last class held in Ryssby School was in 1962, after which the building was sold to Vernon Newberry for $7,000. Today (2007), its asking price is more than $500,000.

Arbor Day was celebrated every year by planting trees in the Ryssby schoolyard. "But it was such a dry, windy hill that none ever grew—only cactus," said former student Alice Steele Campion. *Courtesy of Maxine DeWalt Steele.*

Waiting for the Mail

In this modern world of telephones, faxes and e-mail, the joy of letter writing has almost disappeared. We've become too accustomed to the instant response of the Internet.

In the 1800s, however, residents of Boulder County anxiously awaited the stagecoach, afternoon train or the rural mail wagon to bring letters from their families back East. Establishing a postal system to serve settlers along the Front Range was an impressive accomplishment by the U.S. Post Office Department. New settlements eager to establish their own post offices were required to complete detailed forms describing their geographic locations.

Imagine pinpointing your exact position on an 1870s map of Boulder County. Because no highway numbers had been assigned to the few roads of that period, geographic landmarks were used instead.

Hoping to become the first postmaster in NiWot (the town's earliest accepted spelling) in 1874, Samuel Dobbins relied on postmaster Royal Hubbard of Longmont to complete and submit his application. After stating the section, township and range, Hubbard described NiWot's location as three-quarters of a mile south of Left Hand Creek and 150 feet west of the Colorado Central Railroad tracks at NiWot Station. Since a bona fide town had not yet been platted, the application referred only to the Modoc section house and the 150 rural families who would be served by a new post office.

Once Niwot was established and a depot was built west of the tracks, local mail began arriving by rail. Mailbags were dropped onto the depot platform as the train passed through town twice a day. Outgoing mail was hung on a pole beside the track so that an agent could snag it with a hook and bring it aboard. This arrangement continued until the 1930s.

Niwot's post office changed locations many times over the years and was usually just a counter in the back of a store. Young Amy Sherman dreaded driving to Niwot with her father for their mail. It seemed as if every time Frank Hornbaker placed his barn dance ads in the post office window, it triggered loud shouting matches in the street with Reverend Tillman, the United Brethren preacher.

Only when the post office moved from Reverend Taylor's grocery store to the empty bank building across the street did it occupy an entire building. When Howard Morton purchased the building years later, he discovered lists of early postal patrons, along with an 1892 Post Office Department directive outlining the proper disposal procedures for used or defective mailbags and locks.

Postmaster Eva Haddon balances on the mailbag pole as she slips rings attached to the top and bottom of the bag over two hinged bars. When the train passed slowly by, the bag was snagged either by a pole mounted on the railway post office car or by an agent who pulled down on the bag to release it. *Courtesy of Niwot Historical Society.*

Although mailbags are no longer tossed on the depot platform, folks in Niwot still walk to the post office each morning, stopping to visit with friends along the way.

A Childhood Revisited

In August 1921, a short paragraph appeared in the *Niwot Tribune* stating, "Guy Wing is confined to home with illness." Almost seventy-five years later, Guy's son John Wing received a reprint of that newspaper from the

Niwot Historical Society. After reading the paragraph about his father, John remarked, "What an understatement that was."

"My father had caught scarlet fever. It swept our whole family except my mother. And I, being just a little older than three years, almost died. We were quarantined for weeks on end," he continued, "and without the goodness of neighbors, [we] would have starved to death. They would come by and drop food and supplies over the fence."

The only neighbors that John could remember after all those years were the Dehns, the Lippincotts and the Goulds. But there were no doubt many others. From 1918 until 1925, Guy and Betty Wing lived on about two acres of land northwest of Niwot with their four children. It was through their son's correspondence with Idell Leinweber of the historical society that a brief glimpse of life in Niwot in the 1920s was revealed. Following are a just a few of John's childhood recollections.

> *I still remember Mr. Esgar and Reverend Taylor, as my family drove into Niwot in our 1918 Model T Ford and sold eggs to these two merchants. My family was in the chicken business and we raised thousands of white Wyandot chickens. In the very early spring, we would get thousands of eggs and the whole house was turned into one giant incubator. We had as many as 5000 chickens growing up, and when they got to market size, they were harvested like any other crop and sold. This was my parents' main source of income. Our home in Niwot, as well as most of the homes at that time, had no inside plumbing. We had to carry water from a cistern. No electricity. We used kerosene lamps, and burned wood and coal for heating. Such a thing as an inside toilet was just unheard of. I well remember the band concerts in the old bandstand. Charles Dehn was the conductor, and his boys Floyd and Paul also played in the band. Charles played the zither, an instrument you do not see too much of anymore. We used to love to come into Niwot for the Saturday night concerts and my folks always bought us an ice cream cone, a great treat in those days.*

Wing wrote his letters from Fresno, California, where he had retired years ago. He made it back to Colorado for his sixtieth high school reunion in 1995 and visited Niwot for the first time in many years. He found that all of the buildings mentioned in his letters were still standing. Frank Esgar's grocery store building was now Chris Finger's piano store, and Reverend Taylor's grocery store had once occupied the white frame building next door. The ice cream cones he mentioned were scooped from a soda fountain inside the

The Niwot Mercantile was built by John Nelson in 1907. Its walls were constructed of concrete blocks, a fairly new construction material in those days. *Courtesy of Niwot Historical Society.*

Wise Buys building. Only the bandstand, which stood at the intersection of Murray and Second Avenue, was gone.

"The changes were amazing to me," John remarked. "I think it is wonderful the way you have preserved old Niwot."

FILL 'ER UP

It took farmers in rural Boulder County years to trust modern technology enough to trade in their draft horses for tractors in the 1930s and 1940s. The transition from buggies to automobiles didn't happen overnight either.

But as new cars gradually appeared along the narrow dirt roads, hometown newspapers took notice. They chided inexperienced drivers who swerved into ditches, and they tattled on the latest resident to drive through the back wall of his barn as he struggled to master floor brakes instead of reins.

When George Atkinson saw the change coming in the 1920s, he added a gas station and garage onto to his blacksmith shop on Second Avenue. The sale of fishing supplies, candy, tobacco and auto parts helped to keep his business profitable as customers gradually converted to automobiles.

The old Sherman residence next to Reverend Taylor's grocery store became a filling station when Tom West converted it to a Texaco station in the 1930s. Until business picked up, he supplemented his income by delivering coal from mines near Erie to local households for $5.50 a ton. He also hauled water to the many cisterns in town for $1.28 a load.

Sam Harvey was a county road boss when he purchased West's station in 1933. In addition to gasoline, Sam sold Seiberling tires and car batteries. Young Howard Morton also remembered buying candy there on his way home from school.

John Nelson's Conoco station is now occupied by Wise Buys Antiques. Nelson built it in 1907, shortly after completing Nelson Hall across the street. Since his summers were often spent at the mineral baths in Hot Sulphur Springs, Colorado, Nelson hired fifteen-year-old Jack Slater to run the business in his absence.

All the early filling stations in town used hand pumps to siphon fuel from storage tanks beneath the street. This arrangement was of little note to neighboring businesses, but it did concern Boulder County when they commenced work on a Second Avenue street improvement project

The Snack Shack at Niwot Road and Second Avenue specialized in homemade pies, sandwiches and burgers. Chief cook and bottle washer Lois Werkmeister Bennett stands in the doorway. *Courtesy of Jae King Wells.*

in 1994. The tanks had to be located and removed before excavation could continue.

By the 1950s, the Skelly station at the east end of Second Avenue had become a popular destination for delivery truck drivers. Made of concrete block, it housed a two-bay garage and café. Lois Bennett remembers when her brother Ernie Werkmeister ran the station in 1955 and asked her to come from Nebraska to manage the Snack Shack for him. At the time, it was the only restaurant in Niwot.

The early filling stations in Old Town Niwot are gone now, and like all of the original businesses, they left without a trace.

HOME DELIVERY

If the term "home delivery" evokes only visions of the pizza guy knocking at the door, then the term "midwife" probably isn't in your vocabulary. The dictionary describes her as a woman who assists other women in childbirth. And although the word *midwifery* has its roots in the distant past, it is still very much a modern term. Google the word today, and numerous midwife web pages appear—over ten in Boulder County alone.

But these are not the women who assisted our grandmothers in childbirth, and they couldn't possibly have the same stories to tell. Such personal accounts can only be gleaned from diaries and oral histories such as those found in *Voices of American Homemakers*, an oral history project of the National Extension Homemakers Council, published in 1985.

"Most babies were born at home," stated Sophia Bigge. "That's just the way it was. You delivered right in your own bed."

Other recollections came from the midwives themselves. "Around 1927 or so, I began caring for mothers and babies—doing the nursing care, housework and cooking," stated Lora Torsey. "I stayed on a case about two weeks. Then somebody else would want me." Working conditions varied with each of Lora's clients, however. "I once worked in a home that had no electric lights—only kerosene lamps and lanterns," she recalled. "They pumped their water by hand, and they burned green wood to heat the water."

Evelyn Slater often assisted with childbirths in Niwot. According to her son, Herb Atkins, Niwot had no town doctor in the 1930s. "Folks went to Dr. White in Longmont, and a few went to Boulder," he said. "For delivering babies, the doctor would stop by and pick up Mom to assist him."

Julia Gordon was a practical nurse and midwife in Erie in the 1920s. "She attended an awful lot of births," her grandson Dudley Pitchford said. "She

All of Thomas and Georgiana Kneale's children were born before Niwot had a resident doctor. Young Tom, on his mother's lap, was born in 1896, possibly with a neighbor or midwife in attendance. *Courtesy of Niwot Historical Society.*

would go to their houses on the farms or at the coal mining camps, where they lived. She would be there when the child was born, stay for ten days and help the mother get adjusted."

As a boy, Dudley listened as his grandmother described her experiences. "A lot of times she was paid [for her services] in groceries, in vegetables from the farm or often just a simple 'thank you.'"

Part VII

HARD TIMES

ALL I COULD SEE WAS SNOW

Students today refer to snow days as those wonderful breaks from class when travel to and from school is too treacherous to attempt. Years ago, such a term didn't exist, and attendance was expected no matter what the weather. "We went to school just the same," said Cleo Tallman, recalling her days as a student near Hygiene. "We had high overshoes, and we just tramped along."

To Irene Smith and her siblings, deep snow meant trekking to the Ryssby School on wooden skis fashioned by their father. "He made them out of one-by-fours with a metal piece on the front so we wouldn't be sticking them into the snow all the time," she explained. "We took the other children on the back of us with their feet on the skis. It was quite a thing to get the little ones to take a step when we did."

A record snowfall occurred along the foothills in December 1913, when a blizzard dropped almost four feet of snow in just two days. It spawned drifts that reached even higher, and schools along the entire Front Range experienced a well-deserved snow day that stretched into more than a week.

"I remember those big drifts," said Cleo. "We couldn't even see the fences." Her husband, Glenn, chimed in, "I very plainly remember when I was four, walking around the house where my dad and brother had shoveled out a path. And all I could see was snow."

George Poor's father shoveled a path to the barn that became a trap when the family rooster laid claim to it. George resorted to carrying a stout stick to "work him over" the next time he ventured outside.

Thomas Kneale, who farmed east of Niwot, released all of his horses after the
Blizzard of 1913 and herded them to Niwot to trample the deep snowdrifts.
Courtesy of Niwot Historical Society.

Allen and Vera Bolton were inside the Niwot schoolhouse when the
snow began to fall that December day. By the time their class was excused,
winds were already whipping up high drifts. They had driven their pony
cart to school, and it was obvious they couldn't reach their farmhouse
three miles away. Fortunately, Grandpa Frank Bolton lived next door to
the post office in town, so the children headed in that direction. After
reaching his house, they unhitched the cart, fed the pony and tied him
in the barn. Grandma Bolton was ready with blankets and warm clothes
as they hurried inside to thaw out. Two days passed before word reached
their parents that they were safe.

The snowdrifts lingered for days, and many families began to run short
of supplies. Trains were stalled, and roads were impassable. County road
crews labored to clear main arteries as quickly as possible, and road boss Ray
Arbuthnot enlisted August Behrmann to help him open the roads to Niwot.
Dragging wooden *A*s behind their draft teams, the two men finally cleared
away enough snow to make travel possible. An *A* was made from two large
beams fashioned into a wedge and joined together by a crossbeam. Despite
its simplicity, it was quite effective at clearing snow.

HARD TIMES IN THE '30s

It was the 1930s, and Niwot was feeling the impact of the Depression. The bank had shuttered its doors in 1931, causing many local farmers to lose all or part of their savings. Fortunately, James Gould had withdrawn his money just months before the stock market crash because the bank was unable to loan him money to buy cattle. He had switched to the First National Bank of Longmont, which was on firmer financial ground. Others, like Frank Bolton, lost confidence in financial institutions altogether and chose to hide their money in their homes.

Frank's son Clyde Bolton helped many in town who had lost everything by buying their property and then selling it back to them at fair terms when the economy rallied.

Charging groceries until payday had been standard practice for years, but during the Depression, grocers Reverend Taylor and Frank Esgar found that those tabs went unpaid for months as families struggled to make ends meet.

Sales of new farm equipment at Walter Hogsett's International Harvester dealership across from the bank fell dramatically. Yet blacksmith George Atkinson had all the work he could handle as farmers brought in their implements for repair rather than replacing them with new models. The lot next to his shop on Second Avenue was always lined with farm implements waiting to be welded, sharpened or straightened.

The specter of hard times made itself known in other ways as well. Because of Niwot's location along a busy railroad line, hobos descended on the town every time the Colorado & Southern train stopped at the

Nimrod Henry was president and Guy Dodd was cashier for the Niwot State Bank when it failed in 1931. Not long out of work, Guy was soon hired as bookkeeper for a local filling station. *Courtesy of Niwot Historical Society.*

119

depot. "I've seen times when one hundred or so were just riding the freight train from here to there to find work," said Glenn McDonald. "One night I was home alone, and a freight train stopped," he continued. "They got off the train and went every which way. Those that found no meals got back on when the train left."

Naomi Tilbury's grandmother lived next to the tracks and became so afraid of the beggars at her door that she gave up her home. "Lots of times," Naomi recalled, "you'd even see children on those trains."

Walter Kneale, who farmed just east of town, let hobos stay in his barn overnight and saw to it that they were fed. Most were willing to work for their meals, but few residents had jobs to offer them.

THE STILL ON GUNBARREL HILL

By the time Prohibition became law in the United States in 1920, Colorado had been dry for four years and the city of Boulder for thirteen years. Even some of the mining towns in Boulder County had begun restricting the sale of liquor.

George Richart, a Niwot native, was Boulder County sheriff during Prohibition. His eldest daughter, Mary, recalled those years. "Father was constantly battling illegal stills on Gunbarrel Hill and Denver mafia slot machines in the back rooms of local taverns," she said.

The Women's Christian Temperance Union (WCTU) took a fairly militant stand against saloons, but it was not the only group protesting the sale of alcohol. The Ku Klux Klan, very active in Colorado in the 1920s, also tracked down and destroyed illegal stills throughout the state.

During Prohibition, liquor was spirited into the United States from Mexico and Canada. And in Boulder County, there were secret stills (distilleries) operating as well. Some home-brewers experimented with a recipe called Sugar Moon, which called for 120 pounds of sugar beets, fifty gallons of spring water and 1½ pounds of yeast. After being allowed to ferment for ten days at eighty degrees, it was boiled, and the captured steam was then distilled into a moderately acceptable liquor—or so they claimed.

On a much larger scale, the biggest still ever found in northern Colorado operated in the 1930s on Gunbarrel Hill, south of Niwot. Although totally hidden underground, Sheriff Richart was alerted to its existence in 1933 by a suspicious-looking non-operating windmill erected at the site. A raid was conducted by both the sheriff and the Boulder police department that April, and nearly one thousand gallons of liquor and five thousand gallons of mash were confiscated.

Whether Niwot residents knew of this still or how the whiskey was transported isn't documented. But Evan Gould remembered "a big car full of bootleggers from Denver" that often met the train from Cheyenne when it stopped to unload wheat at the Niwot flour mill.

Evelyn Ullery of Longmont, Sheriff Richart's youngest daughter, was six years old when her father raided the Gunbarrel still. A teetotaler himself, Richart used the event to impress upon his six children the evils of whiskey. He brought his entire family to the site to breathe in the stench of its whiskey-soaked dirt floor. "Oh, the smell was terrible," Evelyn chuckled. "That's why I don't drink whiskey."

Prohibition for the rest of the nation lasted until 1933. But in the city of Boulder, it took fifteen special elections before its dry law was repealed in 1967.

A Mighty Wind

Settlers in Boulder County have long endured the volatile moods of Mother Nature, including the Blizzard of 1913, which dropped four feet of snow in just two days. Then there were years when swarms of grasshoppers descended on the county, wiping out everything from crops to window curtains and paint on the walls.

Early diaries and newspapers described deaths from typhoid fever, dysentery and smallpox, which followed the wagon trains during this nation's western migration. Closer to home, Boulder County families recall stories told by elders about damaging floods and forest fires that wiped out entire communities in the 1890s.

Today, we no longer experience swarms of locusts. The deep snows of the last century seem to have lessened as Colorado's climate has moderated, and reclamation projects like the building of Barker Dam below Nederland have mitigated the torrents that once flooded communities along the foothills.

Like our predecessors, however, we still suffer from Colorado's damaging winds. There isn't one among us who hasn't experienced a windstorm that frayed our nerves or damaged our property. While our losses often seem substantial, we should perhaps contrast them with those sustained in April 1912, when eighty-five-mile-per-hour winds swept through Boulder County.

The April 19 edition of the *Niwot Weekly News* included several stories describing the effects of that windstorm. Although Niwot itself was only slightly inconvenienced with an annoying disruption of phone service, there were significant delays in the train schedule due to drifting sand on the tracks.

Destruction elsewhere along the Front Range was substantial. Denver suffered about $100,000 in damage from broken windows, fires and demolished homes. The Mitchell-Monarch Mine tipple south of Louisville was destroyed by fire, and reports from Loveland stated that the collapse of its State Mercantile building was imminent.

All but one of the oil derricks southwest of Niwot collapsed in the high winds, and a Colorado Refining Company oil tank was blown onto the railroad tracks at Sixty-third Street. Crews working under Niwot section foreman Juan Apodaca worked all night to clear the tracks.

Because spring planting had just been completed, farmers reported that their seed had been blown out of the ground, and sprouting plants were completely destroyed. Those taking a more optimistic view of the situation, however, predicted that with a good rain, their losses would be minimal. In fact, they had already begun replanting spring wheat where the damage was greatest.

Bad luck seemed to follow King Blanton, who survived one weather-related catastrophe only to be killed by another. He was fatally crushed beneath his mail wagon during a lightning storm, when his horse panicked and tipped it over on him. *Courtesy of Niwot Historical Society.*

Hard Times

King Blanton, Niwot's rural mail carrier, was injured when the wind caught his wagon and slammed it upside down against a fence. He attempted to keep it upright by standing on the step but was knocked to the ground and sprained his back. The mail wagon was badly damaged, and his faithful horse "Bill" was cut by barbed wire. But both were back to work within days with a borrowed buggy.

Niwot in Wartime

Indian uprisings and the Civil War were the first conflicts to have an impact on pioneers arriving at the foot of the Rockies in the 1860s. Colorado had just become a territory when the Civil War broke out in 1861. Boulder County was not yet created, and it would be fourteen years before Niwot appeared. Still, settlement in the Left Hand Valley had already begun.

With the Civil War draining resources across the country, communities in Colorado were struggling. War contracts provided little benefit to Colorado ranchers, whose beef production was almost exclusively for local consumption.

Many early settlers in the Left Hand Valley were Union army veterans when they headed west. Frank Bolton arrived in 1879, after serving in the Michigan cavalry for the duration of the war. Miles Jain, although born in Switzerland, was a veteran as well, having been wounded in 1862.

After his discharge from the First Ohio Volunteer Light Artillery, Charles Wright joined his brother George in operating one of the first mercantiles in Niwot. Nimrod Henry, who later helped to found the Niwot State Bank and other businesses, tried to enlist in the Union army but was rejected. Because of his small stature, officials didn't believe he was old enough to fight. When he turned eighteen, however, he headed for Colorado just three days after Lincoln's assassination.

The effects of World War I were felt in small towns, as well as large cities, all across America. Factories that had previously manufactured farm machinery were now churning out tanks and field artillery, severely impacting agricultural communities like Niwot. Delivery of new farm implements came to a halt as the nation converted to wartime production. Yet local blacksmiths benefited from this conversion as farmers were forced to repair rather than replace their broken equipment.

The scarcity of gasoline and auto parts was not a problem for Niwot residents. The few families who owned cars and trucks at that time simply

Matt McCaslin was among many resourceful Boulder County farmers who began farming with oxen instead of horses, using ox yokes instead of harnesses. The lead and base pairs were yoked and trained, while the cattle in between simply followed behind. *Courtesy of Irene Smith Lybarger.*

resurrected their buggies and wagons whenever transportation was needed. Almost all rural families were still using draft animals anyway.

Then the army began requisitioning mules and horses to pull heavy artillery on the battlefields overseas. The resulting lack of horsepower back home was solved when local farmers resorted to training cattle as draft animals.

Daily life continued as usual. Food supplies were adequate since most families either farmed or maintained vegetable gardens, chickens and a few pigs in their backyards.

Part VIII

CHANGES IN THE AIR

PIONEER ZEPHYR COMES TO NIWOT

In an October 1949 issue, the *Niwot Tribune* heralded the introduction of diesel-powered rail transportation to Niwot. On October 15, the day before its inaugural run between Denver and Cheyenne, the modern stainless steel Pioneer Zephyr stopped briefly at the Niwot depot so that curious onlookers could see the new streamliner.

Tribune editor Doyle Hornbaker wrote, "This is the same Pioneer Zephyr—America's first diesel streamline train—that made the epochal dawn-to-dusk run from Denver to Chicago in 1934." It had achieved the 1,015-mile dash in just thirteen hours and five minutes, traveling at an average speed of 77 miles an hour.

The Colorado & Southern (C&S) Railway, suffering for years from declining ridership and loss of revenue from its older rolling stock, was betting on success with the modern four-car articulated train with direct connections to the Burlington Railroad's Denver Zephyr and points east. As a disclaimer, the C&S stated that "continued operation of this train will depend on the amount of patronage received from the communities it serves."

Those communities included Denver and Cheyenne, with an optional flag stop in Niwot. Chuck Leinweber remembered paying just a nickel to ride on it from Niwot to Longmont.

The fifteen-minute stop at the Niwot depot that October day allowed little time to inspect the modern amenities the Zephyr had to offer. Its ad in the *Niwot Tribune* promised "new travel enjoyment to this region with restful

Niwot got its first look at the Pioneer Zephyr in October 1949. Its double headlight was added after a fatal grade-crossing collision the year before. The cab was redesigned as well, seating the engineer farther back from the front of the train. *Courtesy of Niwot Historical Society.*

reclining seats and double-width windows in either a comfortable coach or parlor car."

The Pioneer Zephyr route through Niwot lasted from October 1949 to April 1950. In 1960, twenty-six years after its record-breaking dash, the original Pioneer Zephyr was donated to the Museum of Science and Industry in Chicago, where it remains one of its more popular exhibits.

BARN AGAIN

Throughout most of 2002, motorists traveling along Highway 66 between Longmont and Lyons witnessed a historic restoration project of major proportions. The Lohr-McIntosh barn just north of McIntosh Lake was quite literally undergoing a facelift.

For years, the weathered old barn had sagged lower and lower from neglect and old age. But in the summer of 2002, its roofline slowly began to straighten. Rotted boards were replaced, and the once-crumbling rubble sandstone foundation was repaired enough to once again support the weight of the huge structure. After receiving a "Barn Again" grant from the

Colorado Historical Society and preservation funding from Boulder County, restoration of the unique pegged barn began.

Built in 1881, the Lohr-McIntosh barn is one of several outbuildings on Boulder County's Agricultural Heritage Center (AHC) property just east of Hygiene. The entire farmstead was purchased from Neil (Shorty) Lohr in 1985 as an open space acquisition. Shorty's grandfather, George McIntosh, had homesteaded the land in 1868. Shorty loved to listen to his grandfather talk about the past, and those stories were captured on tape prior to Shorty's death in 1991.

George McIntosh lived the life of a true pioneer, from his days as a freighter along the Overland Stage route between Denver and Fort Laramie to his enlistment in Company G, First Colorado Cavalry, during the Civil War. It was during his many freighting trips across the St. Vrain Valley that he first saw the land that he would one day homestead. When time permitted, he pastured his ox team in the natural drainage that is now McIntosh Lake. Years later, he told his grandson, "[The] grass grew high enough [there] to hide a buffalo bull."

Shorty never married. Instead, he chose to remain on the farm where he raised hay, maintained a small dairy herd and, in later years, cared for his ailing mother, Minnie.

It was because of his love for the land that had been in the family for over 140 years that Shorty made a generous offer to the county. Watching

The Lohr-McIntosh barn was designed for hay storage. Spaces between the upright boards, normally covered by battens, were left uncovered, allowing for westerly winds to blow through the side walls, further drying out the hay inside. Research prior to restoration revealed that the barn had possibly been built from a kit. *Courtesy of the author.*

as housing developments spread across neighboring farms, he had no desire to see his land subdivided. Instead, he wanted it preserved as a link to a way of life that is rapidly disappearing in Boulder County. So when the county purchased his farm, he donated back $250,000 of the purchase price to develop an on-site educational center.

Today, the Lohr-McIntosh farm is preserved for future generations to visit and learn about farming practices in the period between 1900 and 1925. Approximately 220 irrigated acres are leased for grazing and haying, while the 6-acre AHC buildings are open to the public for self-guided tours and interpretive programming.

Niwot Adds a New Landmark

When Boulder County created the Niwot Historic District in 1993, nine structures were declared historically significant because of their age, importance to the town's development and relatively unaltered appearance. When establishing such districts, it is rare to overlook an eligible building, but that is exactly what happened.

Although the town's only firehouse was built next to the Niwot State Bank in 1910, few were aware that it still existed because it had spent the last twenty-four years inside a modern building down the street. Many in town knew it in the 1970s and 1980s as Floyd Edmunds's office in the Niwot Auction House on Second Avenue.

Edmunds had built his business where the Livingston Hotel once stood. After the hotel's demolition in the 1980s, one of its outbuildings remained standing. Years before, the abandoned firehouse had been dragged to the back of the hotel, where it was used as a laundry shed. Windows were added, and its shed doors were replaced with a standard-entry door.

Floyd's wife, Carolyn, was intrigued by the humble little shack and wanted it preserved. So it was incorporated within the auction house as it was being built. The shack continued as an office even after Jim Knoch purchased the building and reopened as the Niwot Antique Emporium. The little building-inside-a-building presented a dilemma, however, when RLET Properties purchased the property for renovation in 1997. Realizing its historic value, yet having no use for it, owner Cotton Burden offered the structure to the Niwot Historical Society.

With the help of volunteers, it was successfully separated into six pieces and hauled across the street to be reassembled on a new foundation next

Volunteers reroofed and painted the little firehouse after it was moved. A flagstone patio and flower beds were added, thus transforming the plain structure into a rest stop for weary pedestrians. *Courtesy of the author.*

to the Left Hand Grange Hall. When the Niwot Historical Society applied for landmarking, the county's Historic Preservation Advisory Board unanimously approved the application. However, because the building now stands on grange property, it required a signed agreement stating that the firehouse could remain on grange property indefinitely. Unanimous approval was given by the Boulder County commissioners, and on October 26, 1999, a ninety-nine-year lease was signed by both the grange and the historical society, which paid a token fee of one dollar.

The firehouse is now officially part of the Niwot Historic District, and like the other nine contributing buildings, it bears a bronze plaque describing its date of construction and original use: "Original Niwot Fire House—Built 1910."

HOW TIMES CHANGE

In the days before telephones, folks in the Left Hand Valley relied on city directories to provide the names and addresses of others living in the area. For many years, the Greater Niwot area was included in a separate section of the Boulder City Directory. Small communities like Sugar Loaf, Hygiene, Peaceful Valley, Lafayette and others were listed as well.

Today, phone books have replaced city directories, but they no longer include the one feature that made earlier versions unique. In the 1896 Boulder directory, for instance, individual professions followed almost every name: William Hornbaker, farmer and justice of the peace; Eric Ereckson, constable; John Nelson, carpenter and wagon maker—and so on.

There were fewer job categories to choose from in those days, unlike the hundreds of occupations we have today. Just imagine what the current Boulder-Longmont phone book would look like if occupations were entered after each name. In Niwot alone, the directory would include bankers, merchants, realtors, mechanics, beauticians and healthcare professionals. And what about those people who hold down two or more jobs? Would they rate a two-line entry in the phone book?

The 1898 city directory listed 145 residents living in the Greater Niwot area. Their occupations were limited to just six categories: section foreman, pastor, blacksmith, carpenter, merchant and farmer. As one might expect, most were farmers.

Although the number of telephones had increased by 1916, the Boulder City Directory was still publishing only names, town affiliations and occupations. Yet the number of professionals in Niwot had expanded considerably, along with its population. Women were now included under their own names and not merely listed as somebody's wife or widow. Several were described as clerks or teachers.

For those who were "employees," their place of employment was listed as well. Those referred to as "laborers," however, included no further information.

City directories continued into the 1980s, using smaller type to accommodate the longer listings. One had to squint a bit to read the description of Niwot in the 1940 edition:

> *Niwot is located in a very rich agricultural section, on the line of the Colorado & Southern Railway, between Boulder and Longmont. People in the vicinity are proud of their seven-room school, having twelve grades where the children have the opportunity of taking four years in high school work right at home.*

This 1937 aerial photograph of Niwot clearly shows its original configuration and the agricultural land surrounding it. The railroad tracks bisected the town, but the Diagonal Highway had not yet been built. *Courtesy of Niwot Historical Society.*

Boulder directories dating from 1892 to 1989 are archived at the Carnegie Branch Library for Local History in Boulder. To discover who lived and worked in the early mining towns and farming communities during those years, drop in and see just how much times have changed.

CENTENNIAL FARM AWARDS

Although farmsteads are disappearing from our landscape in alarming numbers, there are still many historic farms in Boulder County that date back a century or more. At last count, twenty-two of those properties have officially been declared centennial farms by the State of Colorado.

Richard Lamm, then governor of Colorado, created the Centennial Farms program in 1986, in conjunction with the Colorado Historical Society (now called History Colorado) and the Colorado Department of Agriculture. Today, the program is administered by the State Historical Fund, a program under History Colorado. If buildings over fifty years of age remain on the property, it also qualifies for an additional "historic structures" award.

The first year, thirty-four Colorado farms and ranches were designated, four of them from Boulder County. In September 1986, families representing the Montgomery, Leyner, Zweck and Wise Farms were invited to a special recognition ceremony during the Colorado State Fair in Pueblo.

"It was nice," Frank Montgomery recalled. "They had a reception in a tent where we all gathered. We had refreshments and then we went to the band shell where they got us all up on the stage." There, the Colorado commissioner of agriculture presented each family with a certificate and a sign for their property, denoting its official historic status.

Today, Colorado has over 350 centennial farms and ranches. In order to qualify for this prestigious award, an applicant must own a working farm or ranch that has been in the same family for a century or more. It must be a minimum of 160 acres in size, or if smaller, it must have gross agricultural sales of at least $1,000 per year.

Although nominations have slowed since the program began twenty-five years ago, sixty-one of Colorado's sixty-four counties are represented on the state's awards list. Some, like Clear Creek and Hinsdale Counties, have only one designated farm each, and many others have only two or three. Boulder County claims twenty-two, but it trails well behind the forty-nine centennial farms in Weld County and the thirty farms in Yuma County. Boulder County's standing is remarkable, however, considering the fact that agriculture no longer drives its local economy. It is not likely to add many farms in the future since eligible agricultural properties continue to be sold to developers for housing or to local governments for open space.

Colorado was the first state in the nation to offer the prestigious Historic Structures Award to families who have successfully preserved original buildings on their farms and ranches. The National Trust for Historic Preservation sponsors this special category, which was awarded to the Alvah Dodd Farm in 1988. Over the years, the Dodd family has preserved many of its outbuildings, including the 1898 brick farmhouse, a large 1910 livestock barn and a granary dating back to 1900.

HISTORY REPEATS ITSELF

When Niwot entered the twentieth century, major transportation issues did not exist. Mail was delivered to town by rail. Travel into the surrounding countryside was possible on roads that presented few problems except during periods of heavy rain and snow. During the Depression, WPA workers assisted county road crews in maintaining those roads.

Today (2007), as Niwot deals with issues surrounding the proposed RTD FasTracks project, it may surprise some that exactly fifty years ago these same issues existed for another project of equal magnitude—one that followed the same route.

In 1957, Boulder's *Daily Camera*, Longmont's *Times-Call* and the *Niwot Tribune* began reporting on controversies surrounding a proposed new highway connecting Boulder to Longmont, paralleling the Colorado & Southern railroad tracks. Funding issues, right of way acquisitions and the impact on business and residential communities were the subjects of many meetings between citizens and what was then known as the Colorado State Department of Highways.

For Niwot, the project meant disruption or closure of roads leading north and west from town and the removal of several buildings just west of the tracks. This included the old Niwot elementary school, which stood directly in the proposed right of way.

According to highway project engineer Laurence Bower, the entire plan was designed in three phases and would take several years to complete. The first phase called for construction of a four-mile section of highway between

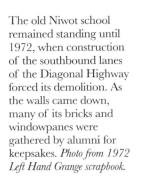

The old Niwot school remained standing until 1972, when construction of the southbound lanes of the Diagonal Highway forced its demolition. As the walls came down, many of its bricks and windowpanes were gathered by alumni for keepsakes. *Photo from 1972 Left Hand Grange scrapbook.*

Boulder and Niwot. The second phase would extend the road from Niwot to Hover Road, and the third would connect the highway to downtown Longmont, still following the railroad tracks.

Phase one presented few problems except for four property owners north of Boulder who refused to sell their land for the right of way. The *Longmont Times-Call* reported: "Final ten-day notices have been given to the four, and if an agreement is not reached, condemnation proceedings will be brought."

Phase two encountered no significant issues, and it was completed for approximately $500,000. Phase three, however, was bogged down in arguments between property owners and the highway department over where the highway should intersect with downtown Longmont. The department's plan to follow the tracks through Longmont to Second Avenue angered merchants on South Main Street who wanted the highway to branch off and connect farther south. A compromise was reached, and the intersection was placed halfway between the two opposing sites.

The Diagonal Highway was completed in 1975, about one hundred years after the railroad tracks were laid.

THREE CABOOSES

Niwot was considered a railroad town until the 1930s, when trains no longer stopped for passengers, freight and mail. After station agent Newton Spangler officially closed the depot in 1932, Niwot was reduced to a flag station. The only trains to stop were those flagged down by a railroad employee. The passenger side of the Niwot station was removed in 1943, and by 1955, the entire building was gone.

Over the past several years, however, three early railroad cabooses have reappeared in town to remind us of Niwot's origins. According to Niwot resident Jason Midyette, cabooses once brought up the rear of nearly every freight train until the mid-1980s, when rising costs prompted railroad companies to eliminate brakemen from their train crews.

A standard caboose was furnished with bunk beds, a desk and a coal stove for heating and cooking. From its cupola overhead, the conductor could observe the entire length of the train. It was quite literally a rolling home and office for the train crew.

Caboose #14649 sits along the tracks just north of Niwot Road and is easily seen by motorists traveling along the Diagonal Highway. It was built in 1907 for service on the Chicago, Burlington & Quincy (CB&Q)

Railroad. The caboose was retired in the 1950s and became a wood shop at the Colorado Railroad Museum in Golden, Colorado. There, its cupola and wheels were removed, and it was painted a pale yellow. Outlasting its usefulness, it was donated to the Boulder County Railway Historical Society (BCRHS) and moved to its Valmont train yard.

Meanwhile, the Niwot Business Association was searching for ways to revive public interest in Niwot's early railroad history. Displaying a caboose along the Diagonal Highway was the perfect solution. A loan agreement between the two entities was drawn up, and the scruffy caboose was trucked to Niwot, where volunteers were waiting to repair it, paint it and rebuild its missing cupola.

Little is known about the second caboose, except that it was bought on impulse and rests on tracks behind the Colterra restaurant at Second Avenue and Franklin Street. Alice Platt, who previously owned the property, discovered the old Colorado & Southern caboose in a field on North Sixty-third Street and relocated it behind her WhyNot Café in 1988. It was first converted into an apartment, and then it housed a series of small businesses.

This CB&Q caboose was moved in 2003 from Valmont to Whistle Stop Park in Niwot by the Boulder County Railway Historical Society. *Courtesy of Niwot Historical Society.*

Caboose #48 arrived in Niwot just like all the others—on a flatbed truck. With the help of a crane, it was lifted over the white picket fence at 100 Murray Street and placed on a new wheel assembly. Constructed in 1908, it operated on the St. Joseph & Grand Island Railroad until its retirement in 1950. It, too, was saved from the scrap heap to become a yard office for two construction-related businesses.

In 1984, it was moved to the Forney Transportation Museum in Denver, where it continued to function as an outbuilding. When the entire Forney collection was moved to another site, the tired old caboose stayed behind, only to be rescued by Jason Midyette, president and co-founder of the BCRHS. It is the only Niwot caboose to retain its wooden roof walk—a flat surface allowing brakemen to move between cars as they set brakes.

Although Niwot's three cabooses are retired from service, they remain instantly recognizable as relics of an earlier time.

PRESERVING A RURAL LEGACY

A casual drive through the countryside in Boulder County reveals many old barns scattered among housing developments and cropland. Having once shared a barnyard with chicken coops, granaries and milk houses, they stand in silent testimony to a once-flourishing agricultural economy. Some still stand next to the farmhouse on an acre or two of land, but most are permanently separated from their original fields and pastures. Surrounded by new houses sprouting like cornstalks, these weathered buildings still catch our eyes and remind us of an earlier time.

The Lohr-McIntosh barn near Hygiene stands next to Highway 66 on land now owned by the county. Built by George McIntosh in about 1875, it has withstood more than 130 years of fierce westerly winds and continual vibrations from heavy traffic only a few yards from its foundation. McIntosh's grandson Neil Lohr described how its cross-timbers were shimmed to fit into holes in the uprights, allowing the entire barn to sway. "I don't think if it had been spiked together it would be standin' there now," he said.

Travelers on the Longmont Diagonal still admire the Dodd Barn at the corner of Niwot Road and Seventy-third Street. Built by Alvah Dodd in about 1910, it once sheltered twenty cows and twenty horses. But today, it stands empty and is in need of repair.

Most early barns in Boulder County were of frame construction. But shortly after 1900, concrete blocks resembling sculpted stone were introduced.

Restoration of the historic Dodd barn by descendants of Alvah Dodd is underway. But because of its immense size, it will no doubt be a long and expensive undertaking. *Courtesy of Niwot Historical Society.*

Farmers discovered that structures built from these blocks maintained an almost constant temperature winter and summer, making them ideal for milk houses and dairy barns.

New owners who appreciate the historic value of old barns may attempt to preserve and repair them. But those who plan to demolish them might be surprised to learn of county historic preservation regulations implemented in 1992. Demolition permits for property fifty years and older must undergo special review by the county's citizen-based Historic Preservation Advisory Board (HPAB), followed by a final ruling from the board of county commissioners.

During the 1960s, more than 100,000 acres of Boulder County farmland were converted to nonagricultural uses, and countless farm buildings were remodeled or razed. To encourage preservation of any remaining historic structures, the county introduced its Historic Preservation Program in 1992. Since that time, scores of agricultural sites and historic buildings have been identified and landmarked in unincorporated parts of the county.

Local incorporated communities have landmarking capabilities as well, allowing their eligible historic properties to qualify for preservation funding from the state and other sources.

INDEX

ABOUT THE AUTHOR

A nne Quinby Dyni has been writing her "Yesterday's News" column
for the *Left Hand Valley Courier* since 1997. As an oral history volunteer
for Boulder, Colorado's Carnegie Branch Library for Local History, she
has interviewed more than 150 individuals, primarily as research for the
four local history books and three videos she has written since moving to
Boulder County in 1978. They include: *Pioneer Voices of the Boulder Valley: An
Oral History*; *Erie, Colorado: A Coal Town Revisited*; *Back to the Basics: The Frontier
Schools of Boulder County*; and DVDs entitled *Prospecting the Prairie* and *Niwot,
Colorado: Echoes of a Railroad Town*.

Visit us at
www.historypress.net